dreamweaver

To Goldy, Star, Isoldé & Olwen, without whom it wouldn't have been written
... and all the gang at the Shapeshifter's Arms

Dreamweaving - the Shaman's Way to walk between the worlds ...

Dreamweaver is a practical workbook which introduces you to the way of the shaman, walking between the worlds. Learn the way to travel the Lands of Dream consciously from a Dreamweaver trained to walk between the worlds and to teach others to do so too.

The exercises are easy to follow and lead you progressively towards being able to dream consciously and lucidly. They also show you how to interpret your own dreams rather than relying on concepts and ideas which may not be your own. You build your own Dreamweb as a practical project throughout the workbook.

The work has been tried and tested with real people since the 1980s. It can bring you new understanding of Life, the universe and your place in the plan, connected to all living beings and working respectfully

There's a strong sense of communion with the kingdoms of nature, the elemental realms and the spirit world.

As the Old Ones tell us, walk lightly and joyfully with the Earth.

Caitlin and John Matthews – authors of *The Celtic Shaman* and *Singing the Soul Back Home* - say ...
  "Elen's book is a delight! Informative, simply written and full of wisdom"

About the Author

Elen Sentier is a practising shaman, druid teacher and transpersonal counsellor. She has worked with dreams all her life and first learned her craft from her father and uncle who also taught her the Celtic mystery tales. Brought up in a magical and shamanic family Elen is, herself, a practising Dreamweaver.

In 1999, she founded Rainbow Warriors, the international school of Celtic shamanism, go to **www.peagreenboat.demon.co.uk** for more information. She is the author of magical, mystery and fantasy novels including *The Owl Woman, Shadow Lands* and *Toad*. Her next shamanic workbook - *Numerology: The Spiral Path* - comes out in 2005. *The Oak Tower*, a mystery tale from the Welsh Marches where she lives, is due out in 2006.

She lives in Britain, in the border country between Wales and England, with her husband, three cats and a host of wildlife. It's a land full of the old Celtic mystery tradition. Elen is also an artist and photographer.

Contacting the Author

The author appreciates hearing from you. If you wish to contact the author or would like to more information about this book, please go to
www.owlwoman.org.

Elen Sentier

Dreamweaver

Shamanic Dreamwork & Journeying

includes making your own Dreamweb

2005
Pea Green Boat Publications
UK

Contents

Using this book

Dreamweaving is very powerful.

The work in this book is set out in such a way that, if you follow it, you should find it works for you. You will find it easier to work with this book if you know it before you begin working. Everyone makes mistakes – this is normal. However you will find it a lot more constructive if you have some idea what it is you are supposed to be doing before you start. Don't take the book straight to bed with you and expect it all to happen for you just like that! Read it through once, over a cup of tea, when you are not trying to work. Then please read through each section and make sure you know what you are about to do before you begin. In some places you have to make a tape for yourself of the instructions. You also have to collect and find physical things.

There's space for you to write your own notes at the ends of chapters and within the sections. It's a very good idea to do this, it helps you to make the work your own ... not mine, not a clone of me but yourr own. Powerful work is never done by learning-by-wrote, it always comes from the inner knowing you get from personal, practical experience. However well I write the instructions, and however well you follow them, you will never do things the same way as me ... you're not me! You will take them in, first by reading them then by doing them, and over time they will become your own versions. This is good, it helps the work to evolve over tim, as it should. we none of us live in ancient times, or even yesterday, we live in the Now, our own now, and we can't go backwards. So grow the work through your own practice, making notes will help you do this.

Protection

Protection is important, it's a boundaries thing. It's also about taking on the responsibility for what you do. To do this you need to have a clear sense of your working space, of who you are and who you are not, of working as an equal with Otherworldly beings. Protection encompasses all these things and it's your responsibility to learn to work safely. If things get messy it isn't just you who can be damaged - you can harm Otherworld by being thoughtless and clumsy too, so you need to learn all these things, Otherworldly etiquette.

The first and last rule of learning etiquette is ASKING, learning to *ask*. You ask who things are, what they are, why they are here, if they can help you, how they can help you – interview techniques, you might say. You never, absolutely never, just go along with something because it appears impressive, powerful, kindly, beautiful, angelic, like a "master", god-like, friendly or fun. I cannot stress this enough.

As an example, in one of my own dreams I arrived in this grove where a "witchy-looking" woman appeared out of the trees opposite and crooked her finger at me indicating I should go with her. I asked her who she was and she immediately did a transformation into Ceridwen (one of the Celtic 'goddess' figures) and said "Now do you know me? Now will you come?". I said to her "Yes, I know you but why are you here? Are you here to help me with the purpose of my dream?". She smiled at me and said "No. I just wanted to see what you'd do! Go on now, on your way, without me." We smiled at each other and I got on with my dream.

What this example says is that although this was a powerful goddess, and one who has been with me since I was a child, I still had to ask if she was there for my purposes and, when she said no, to refuse to go with her but continue on my own. I asked, questioned, and so kept my boundaries, my power and my intention and was able to do what I had set out to do. Now you are going to have to learn this too and it takes practice like everything you learn. But begin now, before you go any further in this workbook. Remember that to ask, at every stage of your work, is the best protection you can have.

You will find there is a lot of work to do before you begin to actually work with your dreams, to go on magical dreamings and to weave dreams. This preparation work is extremely important and you cannot just dive straight into your dreams and get going without doing it. For one thing it won't work. For another it can be dangerous not to be prepared. You may call up more than you are, as yet, ready to handle and you won't have any idea of what to do.

Imagine being given a bus or a great lorry and told to drive it from London to Rome – and you can't even ride your bicycle without the trainer wheels on yet! This is how it is working with dreams. You have to have driving lessons before you can do it. People get frustrated with this in everyday life but they still have to learn as you do now. How fast you learn is up to you – and it isn't wrong to be either fast or slow, you should go at your own pace. But the steps, exercises and route through this workbook have *not* been laid out to annoy you, they come from practical experience which has worked for a very long time. They also help you to integrate your dreaming into your everyday life. This is what magical dreaming is about, not translation and academic study but practical, useful work to help you walk between the worlds.

Dreaming magically, is about walking between the worlds, finding your own way through the Enchanted Forest, weaving your own dream – and living it.

It is *not* about dream interpretation. There are plenty of books which will give you their own version of the meaning of the various things you meet or which happen in your dreams. While they can be very helpful it is important to remember that they are only one person's view, one person's meanings – and that person isn't you. Other people's perspectives are invaluable as an aid but they are not good foundations for your own life. To follow someone else's view is to live their life. To integrate other views into your own life – if and when they fit – is more constructive.

I have been working with people and their dreams as a shaman, and through psychotherapy and counselling, for many years. Often when people draw their dreams the picture is quite mandala-like, or similar to prehistoric cave paintings, labyrinths or mazes, or intricate drawings from some eastern cultures. They are often more of a "map" of the story than an artistic impression.

Some years ago I began three-dimensional building of these story-maps for myself. Then I began encouraging clients and students to do so too. It was even more powerful than drawing. The "Dreamwebs", as I call them, express each individual's own personal dream life and imagery. Because of my British/Celtic heritage my imagery comes from that perspective but there are many correspondences with other traditions around the world. The Many Coloured Land, as the dream world is called, is not exclusive to any tradition but inclusive of all.

This journey-book offers you ways to work with your dreams which go beyond many of the psychology traditions.

Dreams are far more than projections and/or figments of your personal imagination although they certainly include and are relevant to your personal life and experience. They are often called the "language of the soul" by those who work with them and this takes us well beyond the personal and into what many call the "transpersonal". But even this is still not touching into the realms where dream weaving takes place (beyond self or Self).

Dreams take us to the farthest reaches of imagination.

4

What are Dreams?

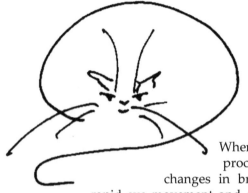

When we sleep many physical processes happen including changes in breathing, brain-wave rhythms, rapid eye movement and sometimes limb movement. To us, it can seem that we move from one realm to another, from one state of consciousness to another, and this is indeed what we do.

Dreams have been recorded going back 10,000 years and maybe more. They are revered and used by many peoples all over the world now as in the past. In modern western society Freud and Jung were pioneers in bringing the usefulness of dreams back to people who had lost the old knowing. However, even they did not go as far as many of the older traditions had done.

Shamanic dream weaving takes you into what is called the Many Coloured Land, the dream world. You could like this to the idea of "potential" in quantum physics – anything is possible there, although not everything may come into being. There really are no limits to the dream world, the only limits are what we are able to allow at any one time. The limits are within us.

In spiritual work, stretching limits is often thought to be "a good thing", but it is also important not to stretch them at the wrong moment or too far. Quite often any blocks you have are there for a very good purpose. They may well have been put there by your soul to stop you "burning our fingers" or "clod-hopping about" in the dream world and trampling things because you are not yet able to see them. You have to learn your way about, how to behave, what the sign-posts mean, so that you can interact with the other Beings you meet there.

Dreams are a place where you can meet and interact with Otherworld Beings. The TV series "Babylon 5" is a good, although limited, model of the Interface between the dream worlds. Babylon 5 was a space station set at a junction, a nexus, of "gates" to other parts of space. It was completely "multi-species". The idea in the series was that it should be a "safe place" where everyone could meet, but of course it wasn't. All sorts of mayhem, intrigue and love affairs went on there.

The Many Coloured Land is like that too. Any and all sorts of being come there, not just humans and not just what humans can imagine either which is why our dreams can be so very incomprehensible! Not all of these Beings have a "friendly" intent towards the others around them, including us. In that way dreams are like Life here in the waking world, where it isn't all safe and not everyone loves us. But the dream world is not all bad either. Usually when we dream the worst thing that happens is we remember only a muddle or nothing at all. If you follow the work through this book you will find that you are able to remember more and more of your dreams.

Your Notes

Dream Weaving

Dreaming is spinning the threads and weaving the strands of Life into a tapestry, a pattern, which makes sense.

Shamans of every persuasion, throughout the ages, have used dreams to walk between the worlds and magical, conscious dreaming is like journeying. As the shaman learns to dream consciously so s/he learns to make choices in the dream, to be able to interact. The exercises through the book will help you to enter dreams knowingly and retain conscious awareness all the way through the dream so it becomes a magical journey.

The "dream" takes place within the three spheres which make up the Many Coloured Land –

LOWERWORLD, place of the *Ancestors*, where all knowing is stored:

UPPERWORLD, place of *Ideas* powers, archetypes, gods/goddesses

MIDDLEWORLD, the place of *Action* manifestation and change.

The Many Coloured Land contains everything. The "places" within each of these worlds are "archetypal" and show themselves in a way which is best suited to your own culture and tradition.

The Powers are not stupid, they are well able to know what forms you find most acceptable – like Arthur Rackham, punk rock, mediaeval, North American images, pre-historic, Hippie, etc.. and use those images in order to communicate with you. The "Beings" you meet, friends, playmates, tricksters, teachers, healers, weary ones whom you can help, the dead who are lost, the young ones who wish to learn from you, are all part of the Many Coloured Land although they will also have counterparts within you. They can assume any shape they wish to attract your attention.

The Land and the Beings all exist *outside* of your consciousness *as well as* within it. Don't forget that.

For most of us, when we sleep, we lose all control and just are "taken". It doesn't have to be this way. If you like to research back through any tradition in the world you will find some mention of the "initiates", "priests", or whatever that tradition calls them, being able to retain conscious awareness as they pass into sleep, and again when they return to wakefulness. This is what magical dreaming is about – dreaming consciously.

It is the crossing of this threshold between waking and sleeping, in either direction, which gives the most trouble. This is where people lose the dream, forget. In alchemical lore and also in Faerie stories one of the most common tales to describe this is the one of going to the castle of the Faerie Queen.

The Seeker goes out and finds a path which leads him deep within the forest. Somewhere along the path he meets someone, often an ugly person which may be male, female or indeterminate, who tells him of the wonders of the Faerie Queen's castle and points out the way there. After various adventures the Seeker arrives at the castle. He is led in, welcomed as though long expected, feasted, entertained and, in some stories, he beds and gets with child the Faerie Queen. After the prescribed time, the Seeker has to leave and the Faerie Queen gives him a bag of Faerie gold to take home. He arrives at the borders of Faerie and as he crosses over he feels his vision change. On arriving home he opens the bag of Faerie gold and finds it is only stones.

Our dreams are like this at first. When we wake we find that although we vaguely recall wonderful things we can't really remember them and when we try to tell them or write them or draw them they seem very dull and ordinary.

Now, in some of the stories, the Seeker goes out again and with even more difficulty finds his way back to Faerie. Often this time he is not welcomed and has a struggle to get in. Eventually he gets the bag of gold again, sometimes by stealing it, but through his trials in the land of Faerie he has learned how to keep the gold, how to stop it from turning back into stones when he crosses the border.

The Seeker comes home changed. Sometimes it is as though he has had a hundred year sleep and no-one recognises him. He is *more, larger,* than when he set out. The Seeker has the Faerie gold and knows how to use it.

Magical dreaming is like this. It's worth thinking now if this is what you want for you will never be the same as you once were if you begin this path. Not everyone feels the rewards are worth the effort. Think carefully before you decide to go on.

Your Notes

Getting Ready to Dreamweave

Your first lesson is to learn to journey out loud, using a tape recorder to record the journey, before learning to dream consciously. This process will help you to achieve conscious awareness while you dream. You will not dream aloud but the experience of learning to speak while journeying really enhances your ability to maintain your awareness when crossing the worlds. It also helps you to learn to speak to Otherworld Beings in an ordinary way, not being pretentious. In my experience Otherworld gets very tired of being "worshipped" by self-negating acolytes who seem always to be so "humble". They are usually so "Heavenly" they are no "Earthly" use!

It is very important to get a good relationship with Otherworld before you begin conscious dreaming so that you believe your dreams rather than trying to explain them away. This process of journeying aloud helps you to *know* Otherworld is real.

Also you *will not* remember everything when you journey, any more than you do when you dream, until you have trained yourself to journey and later to dream consciously. The mind can be wonderfully selective over what it wishes you to remember. The tape gives you a verbatim record of what happened on your journey which will help you believe and stop your everyday mind trying to convince you it's all a figment of your imagination!

Hearing yourself speak on tape reassures you that you were really there. You hear the tone changes in your voice and when your voice is borrowed by Otherworld Beings to speak to you. That re-evokes the journey for you and this is important, especially at the beginning, until you are used to the process and feel at home with it. It's quite possible to get over the "awful" feeling of hearing your own voice, once you get used to it you won't notice yourself at all.

I always use the tape when I journey to make sure I don't miss anything – particularly the "awkward" things that my conscious mind might prefer to forget! Also, listening to the tape again will bring more things to light each time – you need to learn how to encompass the larger reality, piece by piece, and not choke yourself with over large dollops!

The Kit

You need –

•   CD OR TAPE OF DRUMMING or some other rhythmical but *not* tuneful, sound.

In order to journey more easily most shamans and magicians of all sorts use a rhythmical sound which lulls the conscious mind out of its controlling position and allows the other parts of ourselves, such as the feelings, the intuition and the physical body more space in which to work and speak to us.

The four parts of the human personality, the four functions as Jung called them, or the four subtle bodies as many occult traditions say, are Beings, in their own right within us. There is an exercise on how to work with them a bit later on but for now we want to get on with the kit you need to assemble.

Many shamans use drumming and there some excellent tapes and CDs about. However, I also use a CD of gongs, or Tibetan bowls (many Tibetans are also shamans), or a tape of the sea or a stream. All give me a rhythmical continuous sound which helps my "conscious" mind to go off and play, leaving the rest of me open to walking between the worlds.

Whatever you decide to use it is very important that it lasts for NOT MORE THAN half an hour AND that it gives you some sort of "Call Back" signal. You must not go off for hours and have no easy way back. If you let yourself be self-indulgent in this you are just continuing your old habits of not dreaming consciously, not finding your way back across the border not being able to keep your gold from turning into stones.

However, if you decide to adapt a recording of the sea, a stream, gongs, rain or whatever you will need to re-tape it and add your own Call Back. Use the following words –

Soon, now, it will be time to return to the everyday world.
Come home .... Come home .... Come home
Find yourself .... back in your own Sacred Space,. in this world
Now ...... you are back in your own Sacred Space
Soon ...... you will open your eyes and find yourself in your own place
Very gently ...... open your eyes
You are at home ...... you are at home ...... you are at home

Make your own voice gentle, sing-song, at first and very soft so that you don't jolt yourself back. Use the pauses to give yourself time to come back. Gradually let your voice get louder and firmer in tone until finally you tell yourself, quite definitely, that you are now back in everyday space.

You can use a drum to help you. At the firs three "*come homes*" sound the drum (not *too* loud) "Da-da, Da-da, Da-da". Then, at the final three "*You are at homes*" do a single, louder "Da, Da, Da".

- TWO TAPE MACHINES – little portable ones are fine.

  ... one with HEADPHONES to play your drumming tape, so the sound of the drumming does not drown out your words when you talk into the tape for your journey record. And ...

  ... one with a MICROPHONE to record your voice as you speak out your journey.

  Set them up near you. Small battery operated portable ones mean you can work outside easily if you wish. Always test everything and take spare batteries. Test it to check it will hear you even if you talk quietly which you may well do on the journey. So much "technology", isn't it – but it really does help, especially if you are on your own.

- COVERING FOR YOUR EYES – Many people use a scarf. It can be plain white or black or you may find that you are drawn to a particular colour or pattern.

I was given a silk one, hand-painted with owls and the moon. This is very special to me as the Owl is a form of Blodeuwedd, one of the major Celtic empowerers who teaches us the secrets of dreams and the Many Coloured Land, who helps us all in walking between the worlds. Owl is the Night-eagle in some traditions. Also this scarf was a gift – which is very important in this work. You will find that a lot of your *paraphernalia* (working kit) is gifted to you as well as what you make for yourself. It really is nothing like as expensive to be a shaman as some of the adverts in the glossy magazines would like you to believe!

- CANDLES, INCENSE, A STONE AND A BOWL OF WATER, representing the four elements fire, air, earth and water.

- Cushions, blankets and something comfortable to lie on.

- SPACE where you will not be interrupted – most important

Your Notes

Preparation

Preparation and follow-up are very important in all magical work – particularly dreaming. Lack of preparation and follow through is a primary cause of the difficulty people have in remembering their dreams. Additionally they have no sacred space and no guardian/Familiar to help them, nor a Teacher.

So the first things you will learn are –

1. building your **Sacred Space**
2. finding your **Beginning Place**
3. meeting your **Familiar**
4. meeting your **Teacher**

You are getting together a "back-up" team who will help you and guide you in your work of magical dreaming. And you are learning a safe process by which you can enter dreams and return from them bringing the wisdom you've gained back with you.

The ancients of all traditions taught this process of *ritual* for good reason. It sets a pattern, it changes your inner and outer consciousness, it honours, admits and recognises Otherworld as a "valid reality". And it is respectful – respect is vital in all magical work across the worlds.

Preparation is like making a date or appointment in your diary. If you want to meet with your boss, client, bank manager, boyfriend, doctor, plumber or have your car serviced you make an appointment. This means whoever you are going to see has time set aside for you, they can prepare for your coming, or coming to you. Very likely you will have given them some idea of what the meeting is to be about so they can get their things together. You will have some idea of the time needed for the appointment so you, and they, can plan the rest of their day.

Do you drop in on Otherworld as though you were going to borrow a cup of sugar?! Do you think they have nothing else to do but be at your beck and call? Of course you don't! But it's not too often that books put it quite like this. I don't expect ordinary Middleworld people to make space for me at the drop of a hat, unless it's an emergency. Even friends like to have a life beyond me! Similarly Otherworld should be treated with the same respect. Yes, if there really is an emergency they probably will come and help but I don't expect them to drop everything and "answer the phone" just because it's *me* calling!

Preparing the Physical Space

Preparing your physical space is common to all magical work. It is part of the respect I spoke of earlier but has another use as well. By cleaning the space you take notice of it, change it in an occult fashion as well as a physical one. You begin to open the way across the worlds.

You need to have a process to do this and a checklist so you don't forget things, here is one –

- PHYSICAL CLEANING. Yes, it is important that your room, grove, garden, wherever you work is physically clean. If it's a room, as for most of us it has to be, then use the vacuum cleaner and duster, clean the windows. Imagine your favourite boyfriend or girlfriend is coming and get it *that* clean! It's good to try to set aside a particular place for your magical working, even if it has to be used for other things as well. That will help you remember to keep it reasonably clean all the time. If you're able to work outside then again you need to be clean. Bits of dog and cat shit are not usually acceptable within the space, dead leaves, worms, dead flower heads and spiders may well be – but check (see 2 below). You need "clean" not sterile!

- CHECKING - Very simple, but you will need to get used to it. You *ask*, you say something like *"should this be here for the magical work I am about to do?"* – and then you listen with all your senses, not just your ears, for the answer. You are asking the spirits of the place, the gods you will be working with and your Familiar. Even if you don't know them yet, they know you and are listening! Some answer will come into your head, some idea of yes or no. It may be a feeling, the sense of a wind on your skin, a flicker of light, a shiver, hair standing up, cold, hot. It may even be a voice in your head, or in your ear. The Otherworldly Beings use all our senses to try to get through to us!

A friend of mine who was deaf in one ear always found that his Familiars and spirits spoke to him through that ear! And there are many stories of seers who have lost a physical sense having that particular sense as the one which spirit uses as their medium. One of the famous ones is Tiresias, the Greek seer who was blind.

- MAKE SURE YOU HAVE ALL THE EQUIPMENT you need – your tapes, tape recorders, headphones, microphone, eye covering, cushions and blankets, incense or oils, candles, stone, water. See the basic list of Kit above, make your own checklist and use it! Make sure there is water for you to drink. Have a box of tissues near. Make sure candles are safe. And the incense burner! If you have "special objects" you like to have near you, get them.

You need to be real and practical in your dealings with Otherworld. Remember how careful you were as a child when preparing a game, how everything had to be collected and gathered and made just right? You knew then – remember now and do it again now.

- LYING UNDER A BLANKET is an age old way, used in the Celtic tradition, to "contain" us. The Takla mummy finds in China were wrapped in beautiful tartan cloth, so it seems that our ancestors used blankets and ceremonial woven robes as well hides and skins. Tartans have long been associated with "clan" and *clan* in magical work is a traditional *grouping of like souls* as well as those of one blood.

Lying under the blanket is like being inside something, gives us boundaries, like a shell flask, womb, space ship, in which we "travel". So get comfortable, arrange your cushions, futon, sofa, bed, whatever suits you. Make sure you are going to be warm enough. You lose heat when you lie still and you use energy in journeying so have the radiators on or a fire if necessary. Make sure the fire is safe!

Your Notes

The Interface

Preparing the spiritual space – You have made the physical space in which you are going to work sacred, consecrated to your work and showing the respect you feel for Otherworld. Now you are going to prepare and open the Otherworldly space which co-exists with physical space.

I call this the Interface.

The Interface is where the worlds cross over, where they both exist at the same time. The double-ended tree in the picture is a Celtic way of showing this, the roots and branches interweave to form the Rainbow Bridge which contains the worlds.

The branches represent Upperworld.

The roots represent Lowerworld.

The central trunk represents Middleworld.

You create this space when you invoke the seven directions North, East, South, West, Above, Below, Within by walking around the space where you are going to work deosil, sunwise, the way the sun goes round the Earth. If you are in the southern hemisphere you begin at the South, still going deosil, otherwise it is the same.

This "opens" the space, like a lens opening in your eye or in a camera. This drawing of the Hourglass Nebula expresses the idea particularly well. When this is done the spirits of the directions hold the sphere for you while you work. You have created a "meeting place" where the two worlds can come together and interact. This is one of the most important magical acts any human can do and it is *not* one that can be done by the Otherworld Beings. They need us for this. This sort of "working space" can only be created from the pole of the everyday world. Otherworld Beings create gateways through which they can come into our world and through which we can fall into theirs but these are different from this space where *both* worlds exist together in the same space/time frame. This is a very magical place.

When you have made your Dreamweb you will have made a physical representation of this space. It may look something like the double-ended tree, or perhaps remind you of the hourglass nebula. your own three dimensional concept of the Interface. But your dreamweb is a *tool* in the same way as magical wands or staffs, crystal balls, scrying mirrors and such like are and it will be *yours*.

You close this magical space, the Interface, by unwinding it, walking round in the opposite direction, widdershins and thanking the directions for their help.

Your Notes

EXERCISE: OPENING THE INTERFACE

- Set up your altar – in the British, Celtic tradition the following holds good although you will read different elements ascribed to the directions in other traditions.

    Stone in the North holding the energy for Earth
    Incense in the East holding the energy for Air
    Candle in the South holding the energy for Fire
    Water in the West holding the energy for Water

- Set out your place to lie down, with your blanket, eye covering and all the *techyknowledgy*.

- Stand in the North, breath deeply in *and* out, quiet yourself and say aloud

    Beings of the North, I greet you and invite you into this place.
    Guide me, guard me, keep me in the work I am about to do.

- Stand still. Listen to the silence and sounds around you and within you. When you feel it is time, walk around to the East, breath deeply in *and* out, quiet yourself and say aloud

Beings of the East, I greet you and invite you into this place. Guide me, guard me, keep me in the work I am about to do.

- Stand still. Listen to the silence and sounds around you and within you. When you feel it is time, walk around to the South, breath deeply in *and* out, quiet yourself and say aloud

    Beings of the South, I greet you and invite you into this place.
    Guide me, guard me, keep me in the work I am about to do.

- Stand still. Listen to the silence and sounds around you and within you. When you feel it is time, walk around to the West, breath deeply in *and* out, quiet yourself and say aloud

    Beings of the West, I greet you and invite you into this place. Guide
    me, guard me, keep me in the work I am about to do.

- Stand still. Listen to the silence and sounds around you and within you. When you feel it is time, walk back to the North. Then turn and walk into the centre, breath deeply in *and* out, quiet yourself, look up to the heavens and say aloud

    Sky Beings, I greet you and invite you into this place. Guide me,
    guard me, keep me in the work I am about to do.

- Stand still. Listen to the silence and sounds around you and within you. When you feel it is time, breath deeply in *and* out, quiet yourself, look down towards the earth and say aloud

    Earth Beings, I greet you and invite you into this place. Guide me,
    guard me, keep me in the work I am about to do.

- Stand still. Listen to the silence and sounds around you and within you. When you feel it is time, breath deeply in *and* out, quiet yourself, sense inwards to the centre of your own being and say aloud

I greet you, my own soul, and acknowledge you within me. Guide me, guard me, keep me in the work I am about to do.

- Stand still. Listen to the silence and sounds around you and within you. When you feel it is time, breath deeply in *and* out, quiet yourself and walk back out of the space to the North. Let go of the ritual. You are now ready to begin your exercise.

Do this before each exercise or any other working that you do.

Your Notes

At the end of your work or exercise you do a similar closing invocation. You close the space in which you've been working by thanking the seven directions again – in reverse order, Within, Below, Above, West, South, East, North, going widdershins, the opposite way to which the sun goes round.

- Begin at the centre and say
  "Thank you, my own Soul, for guiding, guarding and keeping me in the work I have just done."

- Look to the earth and say
  "Thank you, Earth Beings, for guiding, guarding and keeping me in the work I have just done."

- Look to the heavens and say
  "Thank you, Sky Beings, for guiding, guarding and keeping me in the work I have just done."

- Turn and walk to the West and say
  "Thank you, Beings of the West, for guiding, guarding and keeping me in the work I have just done."

- Turn and walk to the South and say
  "Thank you, Beings of the South, for guiding, guarding and keeping me in the work I have just done."

- Turn and walk to the East and say
  "Thank you, Beings of the East, for guiding, guarding and keeping me in the work I have just done."

- Turn and walk to the North and say
  "Thank you, Beings of the North, for guiding, guarding and keeping me in the work I have just done."

Do this at the end of every working.

When you have finished clear the place physically. Pack up your altar kit in a special bag or box. Clean up any ash. Pick up your bedding, blanket, scarf, shake them out and put them away. Mark the tape of your journey with the day and subject and put it away. Put your drumming tape away and pack up all the *techyknowledgy*. The place should be physically free of your journey.

Sleeping Space

Prepare your sleeping space in a similar way before you go to bed and close it in the morning when you get up. You are probably getting the idea that all this dreaming stuff is hard work. You are quite right, it is!

Sacred Space

This is the place from which the dreamer begins the dream journey. It is a very useful place to have in any case and not just for dreaming. In this exercise you build, discover, create, your own sacred space.

You will already have done your Preparation, set up your altar and opened the Interface ... So

- TURN ON THE TECHNOLOGY. When you are ready, lie down, put your headphones on with the drumming tape. Is your tape recorder on to record your journey ...?!

- COVER YOUR EYES. Now, to paraphrase the old children's radio, if you are comfortable, let us begin ...

- SAY YOUR PURPOSE OUT LOUD, 3 TIMES.
  "I am here to walk between the worlds to find and build my own Sacred Space. I ask the Beings of Otherworld to help me in this task"

- Now, LIE STILL. *Feel* your breathing. Don't try to change anything. *Hear* the drumming. *Feel* yourself lying comfortably and safely in your blanket. *Know* that you are in your own room, in your own physical sacred space.

Exercise: Finding and Building your Sacred Space

Allow your consciousness to flow with the sound. You may already find yourself somewhere. As the place you are now in begins to come into focus take note of it and *begin to talk out loud to the tape*. It might go something like this:-

> *"I'm in a grassy place, It's warm. The sun's shining through leaves, it might be early morning. The grass is very green, it's not damp, no dew. It's a small grove, a clearing in the woods, not very wide. There are flowers, yellow, purple. I can hear something – a stream maybe. A bird flew across the clearing. There's a butterfly, so big, so different from those at home ...."*

- Get to know your place. It will likely be quite different from my description above. It could be indoors, by the sea, a river, mountain, hillside, cave, deep woods, pine trees, lake, waterfall, garden, your favourite place as a child, an attic. It is your place.

- You need to be in it alone. This is important. If you find yourself with another being ask them, very politely, to leave. Tell them that you are here to find and build your own sacred space and you want to do this by yourself. Insist, politely, on being alone. It is important to keep your space and boundaries with Otherworldly Beings. This will be your place from which you can journey out and to which you can return safely and to which no-one, not even the gods, can come unless invited by you. You need this space to do magical work so build it now.

- You have to be able to get to your Sacred Space easily and quickly from either the everyday world or Otherworld. There are times when you need a "bolt-hole" and this is it! It's your "home-base", a familiar "anchor" which you can re-call readily if you ever feel lost between the worlds.

- It needs to have a "DOOR", "GATE", OR "BRIDGE" of some sort. It might be two trees, a rose arch, an actual door or gate. It must be something you can close in some way, even if it's only by drawing a line across it. This helps you to know when you are in it and when you've gone out. It also stops other things entering. They know they cannot cross this line or open this door without your permission.

- When you feel you know this place well enough, or when you hear the Call Back signal, find yourself lying under your blanket again.

- DON'T GET UP IMMEDIATELY. Turn on one side and curl up in the foetal position for a few minutes, gently recalling in your mind's eye where you have been. You are reclaiming your body, getting to know and feel it again after you have been journeying out of it for half an hour. Greet your body and thank it for still being there for you to come back to – don't take it for granted!

- When you are ready, gently sit up, then get up.

- Close the Interface.

Clear the place physically. Pack up your altar kit in a special bag or box. Clean up any ash. Shake out your bedding, blanket, scarf and put them away. Mark the tape of your journey with the day and subject and put it away. Put your drumming tape away and pack up all the *techyknowledgy*. The place should be physically free of your journey.

Your Notes

Practical Work

- DRAW YOUR SACRED SPACE, before you do anything else and before you listen to your tape. This is your very first impression. It will change and grow as you listen to the tape again but this first impression will have things within it which you will never recapture in later listenings and workings.

- LISTEN TO YOUR TAPE QUIETLY BY YOURSELF. Hearing it right after your journey helps reinforce the experience and assure you that you didn't imagine it. It is amazing what hearing your own voice, with all the tone changes and inflections of your actual journey, does.

Listen to the tape several times over the next few days – but only once per day, don't over-load yourself. Then, the following week, journey to your sacred space again. You can repeat this journey over three or four weeks. You don't have to be in a hurry in this work, it is much better to take time, savour everything, allow your whole system to adjust. Your body, emotions, thinking self and your soul are coming to a new way of being together. Give it time.

Your next step is to find out what is beyond the door or gate out of your *Sacred Space*. This is where you discover your *Beginning Place* and, as a precursor to this, here is an exercise which will help you to **know** the directions.

Your Notes

EXERCISE: SENSING THE DIRECTIONS WITHIN YOURSELF

Make sure you have some paper and coloured pens or pencils nearby. You may need them at the end of the exercise. Also somewhere to sit down after and a glass of water.

Most spiritual traditions around the world use and honour the directions. North, South, East and West, are used throughout the world but different traditions ascribe different elements and symbolism to them. The horizontal arms on this diagram represent the four directions, North and South, East and West. The vertical line represents Above, Below and Within. So we have seven directions in all, three on the vertical and four on the horizontal.

- Stand with your arms by your sides. Shut your eyes. Imagine your body as the vertical line in the diagram, your feet below, your head above, your heart at the centre. Spend a moment really feeling your feet anchored to the ground, the earth, beneath you. Feel the top of your head reaching up into the sky above you. Feel yourself anchored to Life through your heart.

- Now stretch your arms out to each side. Imagine your arms as the directions East and West. Again feel the stretch, feel your arms reaching out. After a moment let your arms fall to your sides again. Let go of the feeling.

- When you are ready, stretch out your arms, this time one in front of you and the other behind you. Spend a moment imagining your arms reaching out to the North and the South. Then let your arms fall to your sides again. Let go of the feeling.

- Check your orientation Above and Below. When you know that you are on that vertical thread again bring your focus to your heart. Spend a moment imagining it as the centre of your being. You may feel your heart beat more clearly or hear the pulse of the blood flowing through your body. After a moment let go of this feeling.

- Finally, re-check your vertical orientation again, know that you are on that vertical thread again. Now, come back into the world. Remind yourself that you are back in the everyday world.

- Gently open your eyes and find a place to sit still while you digest the experience.

Contemplate what you've just done, don't try to "think" about it, just recall the sensations and feelings. If any images came to you while you were doing the exercise give them a moment and draw them if possible. It's important not to try and write here. Writing and thinking may make you lose the thread of the image and feelings that you had while doing the exercise.

This exercise helps you connect to the directions. You don't just think or talk about them but *experience* them through your body movement. This is "embodying" and is an important part of all magical work.

YOUR NOTES

BEFRIENDING YOUR SUBTLE BODIES

This next exercise helps you befriend the spirits of the four parts of your personality self, which are also called the "subtle bodies" in occult language. These are the body, emotions, mind and intuition and are often taken for granted. Each one is a spiritual and elemental entity in its own right. I'm using the word "entity" here in its primal meaning of "being" not "something nasty lurking in the woodshed".

Each part, subtle body, has its own intelligence and knowing. It can offer you advice and will work a lot better if you consult it about all the things you need to do in order to live your daily life. Also, your subtle bodies can help you to remember your dreams and to work creatively while dreaming, but they won't if you take them for granted. This exercise will help you make a good relationship with your subtle bodies. You should do it at least once a week. As you get more practised you'll find it takes less time.

FIRST, MAKE A TAPE of the following instructions to talk yourself through the exercise. You will need a **45 minute per side** tape.

BEGIN SPEAKING INTO THE TAPE

Make space on the floor. Get five pieces of paper and write these headings, one per sheet.

BODY – SENSORY self
THINKING self
INTUITIVE self
FEELING self
Watcher/Observer

Lay the pieces of paper in a cross, as follows ...
Body *opposite* Intuition.
Thinking *opposite* Feeling.
Observer/Watcher at the centre.

Make sure you have plenty of physical space so that you can move to each place easily.

• Sit in the centre, the place of the Self, and clear yourself of worry and thoughts. Just sit there and allow stillness to come. < 2 MINUTE PAUSE >

• Now, move to the place of BODY. Sense yourself making contact with your Body essence. Ask Body ... how does it view your life at present. Ask for an image, word, phrase, or sensation for your life at this time. Spend the next three minutes listening to your Body. < 3 MINUTE PAUSE >

- Soon now it will be time to leave Body and return to your Centre. Thank Body for what it has given you and say you will return to speak with it again. Now, return to your Centre. Make a few brief notes or drawings to remind you of what Body said. < 2 MINUTE PAUSE>

- Spend a moment clearing yourself of the sense of being with Body. < 1 MINUTE PAUSE >

- Now move to the place of FEELINGS. Feel yourself making contact with your Feeling essence. Ask Feelings … how do they view your life at present? Ask for an image, word, phrase or feeling for your life at this time. Spend the next three minutes listening to your Feelings. < 3 MINUTE PAUSE >

- Soon now it will be time to leave Feelings and return to your Centre. Thank your Feelings for what they have given you and say you will return to speak with them again. Now, return to your Centre and make brief notes/drawings. < 2 MINUTE PAUSE >

- Spend a moment clearing yourself of being with Feelings. < 1 MINUTE PAUSE >

- Now move to the place of THINKING. Contact your Thinking essence. Ask … how does your Thinking self view your life at present? Ask for an image, word, phrase or picture for your life at this time. Spend the next three minutes listening to your Thinking self.   < 3 MINUTE PAUSE >

- Soon now it will be time to leave Thinking and return to your Centre. Thank Thinking for what it has given you and say you will return again to listen with your thoughts. Now, return to your Centre and make brief notes/drawings. < 2 MINUTE PAUSE >

- Spend a moment clearing yourself of being with Thinking. < 1 MINUTE PAUSE >

- Now move to the place of INTUITION. Contact your Intuitive self. Ask … how does your Intuitive self view your life at present? Ask for an image, word, phrase or idea for your life at this time. Spend the next three minutes listening to your Intuitive self. < 3 MINUTE PAUSE >

- Soon now it will be time to leave your Intuitive self and return to your Centre. Thank your Intuitive self for what it has given you and say that you will return to spend time being with it again. Now, return to your Centre and make brief notes/drawings. < 2 MINUTE PAUSE >

- Spend a moment clearing yourself of being with your Intuitive self.　　< 1 minute pause >

- Now, spend the next three minutes at your Centre allowing the experience to flow gently through you. < 3 minutes pause >

- Now, spend a couple of moments preparing to return to the everyday world. Greet your physical body and thank it for being there for you to return to. < 2 minutes pause >

- When you are ready, open your eyes, stretch, breath deeply and move to somewhere comfortable to sit. Take your pieces of paper with you and review them, synthesising the whole experience. Draw, take the pressure off the logical mind and put it into the pattern forming and recognising mode - so using *both* halves of the brain.

End of tape

Your Notes

EXERCISE: BEFRIENDING YOUR SUBTLE BODIES

Next day, do the exercise, following your taped instructions.

● PREPARE YOUR PHYSICAL SPACE as in the Preparation section. You will need to adapt this slightly as you will NOT be lying under your blanket for this exercise. Read the notes for the tape through thoroughly again.

● OPEN THE INTERFACE as you did before the exercise to find your Sacred Space.

● Do THE EXERCISE which you have taped the day before

● CLOSE THE INTERFACE as you did at the end of your Sacred Space working.

● FINALLY, CLEAR THE PLACE PHYSICALLY, Dismantle your altar, put the candles, incense, water and stone away. Clean up any ash. Pick up your bedding, blanket, scarf, shake them and put them away, pack up all the *techyknowledgy* so the place is free of your journey.

What you have just done will help you know yourself.

We often neglect the subtle and physical parts of ourselves, treat them as automatons, don't give them any respect but we still expect them to do as they're told and keep on going. We wouldn't expect other people to do this if we treated them this way! Body, Feelings, Thinking and Intuition usually have the most practical and useful advice for us, far better than what our friends offer in the pub, but we rarely bother to ask them let alone listen to them. This exercise changes each time you do it, try to make it a weekly habit.

Try it. I've found it has changed my life.

Your Notes

Dreamwebs

The Dreamweb is the Interface between the dream worlds and our everyday reality. It is the place where worlds meet, where both realities are able to co-exist within the same space/time frame. Your Dreamweb is a physical representation of the sacred space you create when you open the Interface by calling the directions.

This space occurs in the magic of the twilight zone – the *between lights*, the time between the *two lights*, the threshold between waking and sleeping, sometimes called the hypnogogic state. The *between lights* is the time between the setting of the sun and the rising of the moon – or the setting of the moon and the rising of the sun. The word "twilight" is a contraction of "two lights" – the Sun and Moon are the two lights.

Our *perspective* changes depending on where we are. Awake, in the light of the sun and from our everyday perspective dreams often appear unreal or nonsensical and seem to have nothing to do with everyday life. Asleep, in the light of the moon and from within Otherworld, dreams are very real and everyday life looks insubstantial. How can we see both at once, so there is no split? This is the twilight magic of the Interface, learning to hold ourselves so that we see both at once.

The Dreamweb is your window, door, threshold, ,gateway, jump-gate, star-gate, transporter room. By making it yourself, out of things which hold particular memories, insights, ideas for you and your own dreams, you empower it as a guardian who will help you hold your place at the Interface.

All magical workers make their own instruments – thus you invest them with your own power and make a commitment to work with Otherworld as an active and responsible being rather than just being a passenger. It is a talisman which links you to your guardian spirits and a window between worlds.

There is no window without any frame. It is the container which enables you to know where you are and to navigate safely and consciously between the worlds. Without a container for your dreams you won't know where you are. You will drift between worlds, anchorless, like a ship without a rudder, like the Flying Dutchman who drifts forever at the mercy of wind and calm and storm, having no control over the ship he rides.

The things you put into your Dreamweb are those which are significant to you. It really doesn't work to make your Dreamweb in a "style" created by someone else. Their images are not your images. Their translations are not yours. What is significant to them is not going to be the same as it is for you. This is why I don't advocate taking on a bought Dreamweb, or using the objects and images of another culture 'just because' they seem to have been doing it for ages and you are not sure of your own history.

We all have magic within us but maybe we have lost the thread. Each person's magic is unique to themselves, we cannot work another person's magic.

You will build your Dreamweb gradually as you go though each of the exercises in this book. It may not be complete even when you come to the end of the book. Many people feel they will be adding to and changing their Dreamweb as long as they are alive and using it, it is a lifelong thing which grows and changes as you do. Part of learning to work with twilight magic is learning not to be fixed and rigid in your ideas, to allow continual growth and change knowing that is how life is. Life cannot exist in stasis, set in concrete. Life is never completed, finished. You cannot draw a line under it and say "Done that! Seen the video, got the tee-shirt, licked the stamp!". Even in death, Life continues to grow!

Learning to work in the Many Coloured Land and to cross the threshold consciously in each direction helps you understand the interconnectedness of all life. Your journeys in the dream world are timeless and so assure you of Life's continuity across the worlds, across time. Your meetings with Otherworld Beings open up your understanding of yourself and your relationship with everything else.

Expanding your reality this way can help you change your life. Many people feel a sort of *home-coming* as they recall the child's less rigid view of reality. Some people, however, find the changes quite dramatic. The poet T. S. Eliot said, in Burnt Norton *"Humankind cannot bear very much reality"*

The Australian peoples speak of Dream Time and say that only as much of the world as we (humans) can dream of at any one time can exist. There is a branch of particle physics which says something very similar. We all need to dream bigger dreams.

Your Notes

Building Materials

- Wood for the frame

- Lots of wool, cotton, embroidery threads/silks, string, tinned copper or silver wire

- Pieces of material, all colours and textures

- Beading needles, craft knives, scissors, pliers, sand paper, beeswax polish, scented oils, polishing cloths and old clothes – so you can get dirty in comfort.

- Shells, glass and wooden beads, feathers, ribbons, toys, bows, lace, satin or paper flowers, coloured leather strips, tassels, dried leaves, bones, raffia, pieces of coral, crystals, twigs, berries, fir cones, silk, shiny thread …

Make or give yourself a "FINDS-BAG" in which you can keep safe all the things you collect. You don't have to do all this at once, it will take a whole lifetime. Collecting and treasuring things is a part of becoming intimate with the world around you, in which you live and which supports your life. Once you learn *intimacy* and practice it you will find your whole life changes. Until you become intimate with everything you will not be able to dream consciously. Your Finds-Bag is a beginning of this – like the hero's bag of gold which he is given by the Faerie Queen- keep it safe.

Things may "fall" on you or appear suddenly at your feet. I was walking down the road from my old home in London one day when I looked down and saw a jay's flight feather lying at my feet. I picked it up. The blue edging shimmered in the sunlight. Jays are the oldest members of the Crow (Corvus) family and birds with whom I feel a strong affinity. A pair had visited our garden for the peanuts for several years but never left me a feather. Now they had – as long as I was awake and aware enough to notice!

You will probably be able to find all the basic materials for building your Dreamweb around your home, out for walks, as gifts, in charity shops. Try not to go out and buy expensive things and don't expect to assemble everything at the beginning as though you were baking a cake. It doesn't work like that. Your Dreamweb will ask for special things from you at particular points in its own building, some of which may take a lot of finding. Learn to listen to and hear its voice. The building itself is a journey. Many people believe it is never finished and never should be while you are alive!

Your Notes

Beginning Place

This is the place is where you *enter* the dream world, the reference point. It is also your *way home* out of your dream and back into the everyday world.

Think of an ordinary map and going on a journey. If you don't know where you are starting from there is no way you are ever going to be able to navigate your way to Birmingham! Dreams and journeys are the same.

You may have heard people say *"Oh! I never bother with all that. I just go out and let things flow, let the gods look after me."* Or some such. Now think about that person. How much useful stuff have they been able to uncover and bring back with them across the worlds? Oh yes, they may come out with wonderful sounding tales of the gods they've met and the places they've been, very impressive. But it can all sound rather like a trip, a film. You may end up, after thinking about it for a bit, saying *"So what?"*. Their dream or journey may be no more than watching TV, a relaxation but no help in finding a home, getting a job, helping a child learn, healing an animal, looking after a garden.

Dreaming Magically helps with all of these things. Tripping out doesn't!

The BEGINNING PLACE in the Celtic tradition is often the Tree of Wisdom and Tradition, or the World Tree, Yggdrasil from the Nordic tradition. The dreamer goes into this Tree and the Tree becomes the "entry/exit" point. Sometimes it is two sentinel trees, or standing stones, or an arch through which you pass, or a bridge you cross, so crossing the threshold between worlds.

EXERCISE: TO FIND YOUR BEGINNING PLACE

The following exercise will help you find your BEGINNING PLACE. Make sure you have only one Beginning Place at first or you will get confused. You need to learn the "process".

- PREPARE YOUR PHYSICAL SPACE as in the Preparation section, set up your altar and OPEN THE INTERFACE.

- TURN ON THE TECHNOLOGY, lie down, put your headphones on, set your tape recorder to record your journey.

- COVER YOUR EYES. Now, if you are comfortable, let us begin

- FIND YOURSELF in your own Sacred Space. SPEAK TO THE TAPE STRAIGHT AWAY. Greet your sacred space, look around, note what you see. Spend some time re-membering. Re-mind yourself that this is *your* space, that you can be quite alone and safe here.

- SAY YOUR PURPOSE ALOUD, 3 TIMES. *"I am here to walk between the worlds to find my own Beginning Place. I ask the Beings of Otherworld to help me in this task"*

- When you feel ready walk through whatever the "opening" is out of your Sacred Space and into your Beginning Place.

- BE STILL THERE. Sit down if you like. Look *slowly* around you and note what you see. KEEP TALKING TO THE TAPE. Use all your senses to find out as much as you can about the Beginning Place. What is the beginning for you?

- Do **NOT** GO OUT OF IT. You are only here to look and explore and find out about the Beginning Place. You will go out soon enough, this time is to look and learn.

- When you hear the Call Back, or before if you are ready earlier, return back through your "door", "gate", "bridge" or "opening" – this is your *re-entry-point* to your Sacred Space. *Close it after you* when you are back in your Sacred Space. Spend some time gently recalling *in your mind's eye* where you have been.

- FIND YOURSELF lying under your blanket again. Turn on one side and curl up in the foetal position for a few minutes. Reclaim your body, get to know it again after your journey out of it for half an hour. Greet your body, *thank it for still being there* when you came back! When you are ready, gently sit up, then get up.

- CLOSE THE INTERFACE in which you've been working – going widdershins as you did at the end of your Sacred Space working.

- FINALLY, CLEAR UP THE PLACE PHYSICALLY, Dismantle your altar, put away your candles, incense, water, stone. Clean up any ash. Shake out your bedding, blanket and scarf and put them away. Mark your tape with the day and subject and put it away safe. Pack up all the *"techyknowledgy"* so the place is free of your journey.

DRAW YOUR BEGINNING PLACE. Do this before you do anything else, so you allow what is in your *body-mind* to come out without being "tidied up" by your conscious mind!

LISTEN TO THE TAPE of your journey AFTER you have done your first drawing. Then make more notes or drawings if you wish.

Soon you will be ready to go and meet your Familiar. Even if they come to you before this keep your boundaries, don't be rushed, don't be so excited and impatient to get on that you try to run before you can walk. It is not respectful to Otherworld to rush about being impatient. And they don't respect you for being a "push-over" every time they try to entice you to do something you hadn't planned, in fact they get quite bored with you! You have to grow, see yourself on equal terms with those you meet in Otherworld. This doesn't mean thinking yourself omnipotent or a god or anything like that. It's about knowing that you have certain valuable skills and abilities and respecting them. You also respect the skills of the Otherworldly Beings. No Teacher, Familiar or Otherworld Being enjoys being around a fluffy sycophant! You are different from them, they are different from you. But you both need each other. This is the beginning of learning to be harmless.

Your Notes

Beginning your Dreamweb – the Frame

First you have to discover what sort of wood *your* Dreamweb wishes to be made of.

Willow is very good. It has a special significance with dreams in the British tradition. Willow or Saille (pronounced sally) is sacred to the goddess Brighid, Lady of Fire and Inspiration who has her Fire Festival, Imbolc, the Willow month. She is also the goddess of Smithcraft, Making, creation and manifestation. Saille, is also about "seer-ship", dreams and night visions. Saille is a useful wood to use in working with dreams. Craft implements and paraphernalia made of willow will help with magical dreaming and dream auguries.

Alder is another of the sacred trees of Britain which you may want to use. It is associated with Bran, the great Innerworld or Lowerworld guardian, and so has strong links with the ancestral dream worlds. Bran is one of the primordial and archetypal guardians. He made a bridge of his body so his followers could cross the river Linon. You may feel this "bridging" ability of alder is what you need for the frame of your Dreamweb. Alder has a lot to do with oracular work as Bran's head was a "fount of wisdom". It also has a strong protective element and you may feel this would be what you need.

Hazel is another "diviner's" tree.

Ash trees hold the "keys" of Otherworld as its seeds and make good Dreamwebs too.

As with everything in this work, spend some time in your sacred space and **ask**. You may hear the word, see the tree or, if it is alder who speaks to you, you might see a raven, or a man's head, or even a tower as Bran's head was buried under the White Tower at the Tower of London. If it was willow you might get an image of a smithy, a fire.

You may get another wood altogether, not everyone has to make their Dreamweb out of only the woods I have just named, your Dreamweb may require something quite different. Whatever image or words you get keep asking until you know what it is that's being said. It's rather like doing a jigsaw puzzle, you have to keep working the pieces until you see where they go. Whatever wood you get, go and look it up in both an "ordinary" book, like a Collins Field Guide as well as books which tell about how the wood is used magically.

When you have found *your* wood the next thing to do is to find what shape *your* Dreamweb wishes to be – circular, eight-sided like the eight directions, four sided or any number. There isn't a "right" shape but *there is the shape that is right for you*. It may be three-dimensional or flat. It might be made from a single branch. Don't be constricted to shapes you've seen North American "dream catchers" made. This isn't what you are making. You are making your own Dreamweb, about your own magical dreaming.

Go to your Beginning Place again, via your Sacred Space, and ask to see the shape of your Dreamweb. When you return make a sketch to remind you and begin building it straight away. Don't go any further than the basic shape. You'll be adding to it as you go through the rest of the exercises.

Find your own work-chant to honour the making of the Dreamweb. It may come to you while you are in your sacred space or later when you draw or actually begin to work with the wood. It may have words or just sounds. Just keep singing it over and over. Or let it sing you.

Your Notes

Making the frame

To bend the wood have a kettle of water continuously boiling on the stove. Ppass the branch through the steam from the kettle while you gradually bend it. Waterproof gloves will spare your hands from the steam burn. Bend the wood carefully *listening* to the noise it makes. If you hear a creak you're a bend away from breaking – be patient and keep steaming the wood as you bend it and singing along with it too. Give it about five minutes of steam for one minute of bend, it is a long slow process and you may well feel quite tired when you are done. When you have bent it to the shape you need, tie the two ends down so it can't move then put it away safe to dry and set.

If your Dreamweb is just one piece of wood you won't need to tie several pieces together. It may feel a little strange if you are used to "dream catchers" but stay with it. It's yours. Sometimes, as a single piece of wood, it can look like an animal or a dragon, or even a Roger Dean space ship.

If you have to tie several pieces of wood together ask the Dreamweb to help you with how to do this. Maybe you need wire, or string, thread or cotton. Perhaps you have to glue and screw or nail the pieces into the right shape. Don't be in too much of a hurry, allow the Dreamweb to guide you how best to make it. Remember, the frame is the 'window', 'gateway'. It frames the entrance and exit between everyday and the Interface.

This is your container. Give it time to grow.

Your Notes

Your Familiar

Familiars have had such bad press over the last few centuries that modern-day people seem to find it more comfortable to borrow the language of other shamanic traditions and call them "power animals". This book doesn't do that. The word Familiar, or Familiar spirit, has come down through the ages in Britain and we are gradually rehabilitating it.

Familiars are the Beings, who live and work with us in both physical and non-physical. Most people think of the bent old woman, stirring her cauldron, with her black cat sitting beside her. While cats seem to have the knack of being very good at the job of Familiar they are by no means the only animals who do this! The image of the witch and her cat tends to come from a "demonised" view of wiseards (wizards) and witches, wise men and women. These people have trained themselves to be mediators, to walk between the worlds for their fellows, both human, plant, animal and planet.

Your Familiar is your friend, guardian, playmate and helper. Never dream without them! They know their way around in Otherworld so, ask and listen to them. They will help you find your way and to make friends with locals.

You may eventually end up with more than one Familiar. If you find yourself presented with more than one *always* check them out. Other things can wear the disguise of your Familiar and you don't want these. A𝗌𝗄! *Asking is the key.* By question and answer you will know what you're dealing with. This is taking on your own responsibility, growing up. There's no-one to nanny you, you must take charge and take the risk/adventure - but not blindly! Remember, you can always choose, say no, say later, say stop. You will *realise* this (make it real in your everyday living) by doing it.

In order to work with your Familiar you first need to find and get to know her or him. Please don't call them "it" – they are not objects but Beings in their own right and it is important to begin your relationship from a place of mutual respect. You may find, though, that your Familiar is quite capable of being either gender or both – don't worry about feeling confused, this is a normal and natural part of magical working. Mostly, people get used to it!

You must build your relationship with your Familiar. Take care of her or him in this world where they are less at home than you. Don't neglect them. Work with them and acknowledge them every day, while you do the washing up as well as when you dream! They are part of you now, don't neglect them.

You are working and promising to live with this being for the rest of your life. We are not too good at this sort of thing at the beginning of the twenty-first century. We like to have "short term contracts", "get out clauses", "terms of reference", "divorces", etc. This doesn't happen in working with Otherworld. Humans cannot make the Many Coloured Land conform to the non-committal lifestyle epitomised by that famous firm of solicitors "Soo, Grabbitte & Runne"! If you feel happiest being uncommitted, if you fear lifelong relationships, not getting your own way, having to work hard, suffering pain and feeling helpless in a relationship then maybe magical dreaming is not for you.

Your Familiar is like a hawk or falcon in some ways. You cannot take on a raptor for "weekends", you cannot have "off days". Raptors bond to one person for the whole of their lives and if you are not prepared to honour this bond then you should not go hawking. The same is true of the bond between your Familiar and you. You cannot dump your Familiar on the RSPCA when you get tired of her or him. A Familiar is for Life not just Yuletide!

I'm making this all sound very hard for a good reason, you should not take this whole process on lightly. It will change your life – forever – and there is no going back. Those of us who have done it would never wish to go back. Yes it hurts, is difficult, frustrating and all sorts of things which modern people consider "stressful" but the Joy, the Life … it is very wonderful to be connected, knowingly, to the universe and to be with it all the time. I am never lonely, however long I am away from human company. I always have someone to call on, who will help me in ways no human can. I have no fear of death – although I must admit I hope the dying process isn't too hard this time! – as I know I will have a companion to walk beside me on the dark path and guide my steps.

To live with Otherworld is the most wonderful thing imaginable.

Your Notes

Before – Invocation and Ritual

The following is a three day preparation which works well for most people. Say the words aloud, or sing or chant them, it may be that a tune will come to you as you say them. BUT OUT LOUD, to be heard in this world is important here. Do the following invocation ritual each morning and evening twilight for 3 days before your journey.

I am preparing the way to meet a friend
Long have we been apart.
I invite you in
To live with me, to share my days, to watch my ways.
I offer you all that I know.
I will care for you and guard you here in Middleworld.
I ask that you care for me,
Guide me, guard me, keep me, When we walk between the worlds.
Old friend, I call you now.
I will meet with you at the appointed time.
Wait for me, come to me, speak to me,
When I enter your realm.

- EARTH – Take a handful of Earth from your own garden/window box/plant pot. Thank it for being there, smooth it gently on your face, leave it there until the ritual is completed.

- WATER – Hold a small bowl of water in your hands. Thank it for being there and drink from it. Keep the rest of the water for the ending of the ritual.

- AIR – Light a small piece of incense, an inch of joss stick. Watch the smoke rising into the air. Thank it for being there.

- FIRE – Light a candle. Look into the heart of the flame and thank it for being there.

- ENDING – Wash the earth from your face with the water from the bowl. Rub your hands dry in the smoke. Douse the incense. Blow out the candle and watch the smoke flow into Otherworld. Let it carry these words, aloud, to your Familiar *"We will be together soon"*.

This is a real Birth, where you are recreated and introduced to your forgotten spiritual source and home. It is the return of the Prodigal – and this is good. But it will also be awe inspiring, wonderful, even terrifying, touching the spirit as well as the soul and the emotions. This is Home – this is reality. It includes all worlds. It takes practise to find your feet, learn the language, how to behave. But once you are there you are never alone again.

Remember – stillness; container; companion; story – these are the necessities for dreaming *and* for Life.

Your Notes

EXERCISE: JOURNEY TO MEET YOUR FAMILIAR

- FIRST, PREPARE YOUR PHYSICAL SPACE as in the Preparation section

- SET UP YOUR ALTAR

- OPEN THE INTERFACE

- TURN ON THE TECHNOLOGY. When you are ready, lie down, put your headphones on with the drumming tape. Is your tape recorder on to record your journey …?!

- COVER YOUR EYES. Now, if you are comfortable, let us begin

- SAY YOUR PURPOSE 3 TIMES, OUT LOUD.

- "I am here to meet my Familiar".

- FIND YOURSELF IN YOUR SACRED SPACE. Spend a moment or two reacquainting yourself with it. When you're ready, go out …

- FIND YOURSELF AT YOUR BEGINNING PLACE. Say, aloud,

- *"I am on an Lowerworld Journey and would like to enter",*

- your Beginning Place will offer you a way in. It may also ask for a gift, if so, there will be one near you. Find it, offer it and enter.

- FIND YOUR WAY **DOWN**. At the bottom there may be someone, perhaps by a fire, but maybe not … don't have preconceptions. And there may be a whole host of beasts on your first journey all waiting for you. This is the Underworld, it is often very like our everyday world but somehow has more "sparkle", life, vibrancy. Note everything you see, don't be in a hurry.

- SAY YOUR PURPOSE ALOUD, AGAIN, THREE TIMES – *"I am here to meet my Familiar".*

- Wait! They choose us, not we them! One or more animal will come to you. As they come ASK them *"Are you my Familiar?"*.

- When *your* Familiar animal comes it *will* tell you it is yours. You occasionally get more than one come. If this happens, say you would prefer to make friends with one at a time. Ask **them** to decide who is coming with you, give them time but agree which one is coming with you and keep asking questions until you know.

- Spend time with your Familiar, make friends. You are equal but different, don't treat your Familiar as a god or a lesser being - be adult about it.

• Don't talk your head off! Don't waste your time telling them about your life, what you really, really want, what your problems are – you are not here for that. If you turn yourself into a Vogon you will probably bore them to death with your life history!

• ASK *"Would you like to show/tell me anything?"*. They will take you somewhere, tell you things, show you things. Whatever it is, go and do it. If you feel uncertain at any time say so to your Familiar and ask for help.

• If they give you a gift, accept it. Gifts from Otherworld are valuable, your Familiar won't give you anything to harm you. This is why you spend time checking that s/he *is* yours!

• At the Call Back signal, or before if you are *both* ready earlier, begin your return and BRING YOUR FAMILIAR WITH YOU, don't leave them in the Underworld! S/he has been waiting this long for you to come, don't abandon them now!

• Make your way together back to your Beginning Place. This establishes a *known route home*, very important. Don't forget to thank your place for helping you.

• Find yourself back in your Sacred Space - *with your Familiar*. Spend time showing your Familiar your sacred space, so they know it. *When you are both ready,* return to your blanket.

• FIND YOURSELVES, both of you, lying under your blanket again and spend a few minutes lying together in the foetal position, after all you've both just been reborn! Come back gently and quietly. Honour what you've done and give it time. Reclaim your body, get to know and feel it again after your journey out of it for half an hour. Greet your body, thank it for still being there for you!

• When you are back, sit up gently and draw your Familiar, to anchor your journey in the present. Ask your Familiar if they would like you to draw or write something for them. It doesn't matter if you are not a great artist, first impressions are very potent and this is not about art, it is about making strands of the Rainbow Bridge which anchor you to Otherworld. Gradually, as you build this bridge stronger and greater, you will be able to walk across it easily into the Many Coloured Land.

• CLOSE THE INTERFACE in which you've been working, as you did at the end of your Sacred Space working.

- FINALLY, CLEAR UP THE PLACE PHYSICALLY, dismantle your altar, put your candles, incense, water, stone away. Clean up any ash. Pick up your bedding, blanket, scarf, shake them out and put them away. Take your tape out and mark it with the day and subject and put it safe. Pack up the *techyknowledgy* so the place is free of your journey.

Your Notes

After - Invocation and Ritual

The following is a three day follow-up ritual which works well for most people. Say the words aloud, or sing or chant them, it may be that a tune will come to you as you say them. But *out loud*, to be heard in this world is important here.

Do this follow-up ritual each morning and evening twilight for 3 days after your journey. Ask your Familiar to be present with you during the ritual.

I greet you,
I honour you,
I treasure you,
I welcome you.
Speak to me and I will hear you,
Show me and I will look,
Be at home with me for I will be a home for you.

This is a promise you are making to your Familiar. Remember silence is the watch-word – do not tell your experience abroad, hold it sacred and secret within yourself.

- EARTH – Take a handful of Earth from your own garden/window box/plant pot. Thank it for being there, smooth it gently on your face, leave it there until the ritual is completed.

- WATER – Hold a small bowl of water in your hands. Thank it for being there and drink from it. Keep the rest of the water for the ending of the ritual.

- AIR – Light a small piece of incense, an inch of joss stick perhaps, and watch the smoke rising into the air. Thank it for being there.

- FIRE – Light a candle. Spend a moment looking into the heart of the flame. Thank it for being there.

- ENDING – Wash the earth from your face with the water from the bowl. Rub your hands dry in the smoke of the incense. Douse the incense. Blow out the candle and watch the smoke flow into Otherworld. Let it carry these words, aloud, to your Familiar "We are together now".

Listening to the tape

Listen to the tape of your journey with your Familiar beside you. This is witnessing yourself - something we don't do a lot of! When you have heard it right through, without stopping and interrupting yourself, make notes, drawings.

- Note your feelings on listening to the tape again,

- Ask your Familiar for any comments they may have,

- Relate what is significant to you in the journey to your everyday life,

- Listen to your journey tape several times, each time doing the three things listed above.

Your Notes

Begin a Diary

What is a magical diary? Magicians work in the Middleworld, in its physical form, as well as in Otherworld and you learn this through observation and keeping records. A magical diary has some similarities to a more conventional diary, you make notes of all the things you notice in your life, home, garden, park, space *such as*

- what birds, flowers, trees, insects you saw,

- what time you saw them

- the weather

And then you add the magical side

- Season and Moon phase

- *How* you saw or found the thing – did a bird drop it on you? Is it very unusual? What happened around you as you found it? Were you alone?

- Your emotional process – at that time

- What was happening in your life then?

- Have you dreamed of it recently, or ever?

- Has it to do with your Familiar?

You will find more questions for yourself later as you grow through the work-book but this will get you started. It's like collecting all the pieces for the "story" of how you found this thing or event. You build it into the context of your own life *and* so you find out more of its life – making connections between you and it, building the web.

You magical diary may include leaves, bark, flowers, feathers, stones, fur, bones, whiskers, teeth, bits of plant, twigs, seeds – anything you find, also put in drawings and photos. Don't use clips from magazines, this is *other people's stuff*. It is very important to have the real things which have come to you, pictures you have taken or drawn yourself, rather than someone else's. It doesn't matter if you believe you can't draw well, the important thing is that you have made the record yourself.

Recording helps you "ground" the work and make sense of it. By writing, drawing, collecting you "send out a thread" from your own being which connects to the thing. You also open yourself to "receive a thread" from it into your own consciousness. This is doing the Taliesin story, becoming everything for yourself and you do this by getting to know as many things as you can as intimately as possible. Your magical diary is the record of your *intimate journey* getting to know the Many Coloured Land and its relationships with the everyday world.

Books are beautiful but not always practical when you need to fix a twig, piece of bark, bone or stone, or even a very large feather on a page. A loose-leaf binder, ring-binder or file may be better. You can insert pages easily over time and even use the plastic pockets to keep things in within the binder. You can decorate the cover to show significant parts of the dream world as you go along. A box can hold some of the lumpier things but cross reference it.

Look at old diaries where the writers have drawn and then written around their drawing or picture. You might have a page with a picture of a blackbird, another of a worm, a drawing of a spider which was also out that morning, a description of the dew and how the sunlight caught it and the rainbows in it, a note (and sketch) of where the blackbird's nest was and how many eggs laid – if, *and only if*, you were able to find out without disturbing the pair. A note of how the earth smelled at that time and how the sun suddenly shone out from under a dark heavy purple cloud. You are learning to notice and *see how like* the dream world the everyday can be. You are spinning more strands for your Rainbow Bridge

Your diary will be beautiful. Yes, it really will, even if you currently believe you can't create a beautiful diary. In its beauty it will also hold memories for you – and this is one of its other major attributes. It is a time capsule, full of keys which will unlock the memories of those moments for you in years to come. It may be how you will tell and show others, children, friends, by taking them through "the story" of your diary.

Your Notes

Building your Dreamweb – the Web

You have built the basic shape, you have the wood, polished or not as it chose, and shaped as it chose. Now you will build into it the web. This may be a net-like thing or it may be a piece of material or several pieces of material joined together onto which you attach other things later. You can also paint the material.

Begin by OPENING THE INTERFACE and making your work-place sacred as you do every other part of your life. Invite your Familiar to be with you.

Now take the drawings of your Familiar and put them on the ground near your Dreamweb, Put your other *finds* around near it and sit with them. You are building the web, the strands of life on which you and your Familiar will travel together. I find it helps to sing the chant again then my hands begin of themselves and reach out without me thinking about it and find the right threads.

Once you have the basic shape and idea, join the points with thread/ string/wool. Keep on joining the points until you have made a small shape at the centre – this will be the same shape as the outer rim. It's like having a small window within a large one. Or a small inset screen within the larger screen of your television or VDU. Windows ... perhaps Bill Gates was "dreaming" along these lines ...!

Put beads, feathers, bones, twigs, whatever your Dreamweb asks for at the outer rim where the threads are attached. These are markers, exit/ entry points, places where paths may begin and/or end later. For now, just get the web onto the frame, with the central window mirroring the outer one, you will build more after your next journey.

You can take a single piece of material for making the web, stretch it and attach it to the frame with cord, silk, string, by sewing and/or tying. You might also want to use several pieces of material, tying and stretching them over the frame. Different colours and textures can be very evocative here. Some people find they need to use a plain piece of material and then paint it to show patterns and maybe even pictures of their Familiar, Teacher or other Beings they meet.

Spend the time with your Dreamweb finding out what it wants and what will feel right for you. Don't feel that you have to use "either/or" of these methods. Perhaps your Dreamweb needs both or even quite different ways of creating the web. Do what your instincts and intuition suggest *and* talk it over with your Familiar.

You will end this stage of building at the centre of the Dreamweb, going out to in. This is the time to stop. You have created the Web of Life on the frame of the Interface so spend several days playing with it along with your Familiar.

When you have finished, CLOSE THE INTERFACE AGAIN, clear your space and wrap everything so that it is held together and away from other eyes, keep it sacred and secret. Do not allow others to touch Dreamweb. It is yours and gradually filling with your essence so you will not want others touching you through it, nor is it be good for them to touch your energy in this way. It is for you, attuned to you, not to them. You are not making a healing tool for others, nor something to share in a friendly way. Part of holding sacredness is to learn to have boundaries and to keep them and covering your things is a good primal mechanism to stop people touching. Most people won't touch or unwrap something that looks as though it is supposed to be left alone.

Your Notes

Your Teacher

This is a journey to what some traditions call "the realm of ideas", or "potential. Teachers are planners, architects, builders of thought-forms. William Blake's pictures and words may help you get an idea of this place. Teachers are very different from Familiars, they have a different purpose and perspective on life, the universe and everything. Your Teacher is your guide and friend. They know the plans you made for this incarnation, they were with you when you made them and, now that you are ready to hear, they will help you fulfil them.

Your Teacher – s/he may or may not look like a human – will be found in what we call the Upperworld in the Celtic tradition and you will travel there to meet them. This is a very different journey from the one you took to meet your Familiar.

You may well have found your Familiar playful, earthy and practical. Your Teacher will probably feel more serious and focused on work, although they too have a good sense of humour. They have many other concerns besides you, many other "students" with whom they work and many other things to do as well as teach you. They can sound quite brusque and unsympathetic and although they are kindly it won't be sentimental and they will certainly "kick ass" when required. They won't live with you or spend a lot of time around you as your Familiar does. And they are not *yours* in the same way. They agree to work with you when you feel you are able to work with them and they wait for you to realise that you are ready. Teachers don't come round giving out medals and house-points and promoting you to prefect. They wait and watch and it is you who "initiate" yourself into readiness to work with them. You may not see them every time you dream and you certainly don't need to.

You may eventually have more than one Teacher, each being there for particular purposes in which they are interested and with which you can help them. This is the beginning of your work in helping Life to be. No longer are you a child, a passenger, being taken along and looked after. Now you are becoming adult in more worlds than just the one you were physically born into and so you begin to take on responsibilities for looking after things.

Again *Asking is the key* to your relationship. Someone said a long time ago "the only stupid question is the one you never ask!". Remember Parsifal (if you don't know the story, read it). His major problem was in not asking a question. As soon as he got the message and asked, the Grail came to him. So it can to you. But your journey may take a while as his did. The Parsifal story is very relevant to this work.

Your Notes

Exercise: Journey meet your Teacher

- Prepare your physical space as in the Preparation section

- Set up your altar

- Open the Interface

- Turn on the Technology. When you are ready, lie down, *put your headphones on with the drumming tape.* Is your tape recorder on to record your journey …?!

- Cover your eyes. Now, if you are comfortable, let us begin …

- Say your purpose out loud, 3 times.
"I am here to meet my Teacher

- Find yourself in your sacred space Spend a moment or two reacquainting yourself with it. Be at home.
Call your Familiar to you – if they are not already there. Tell them that you are going on an Upperworld journey to meet your Teacher and ask them to come with you, to help and guard and guide you. They will almost certainly agree readily.
If they question you about your purpose and journey, talk it over with them. If they really are adamant that you shouldn't go then follow their advice, however disappointed you may be. Remember, they know what they are doing. There will be another time.
When you're both ready, go out …

- Find yourself at your Beginning Place. Say that you are on an Upperworld Journey and would like to enter. You will be offered a way in. If you are asked for a gift there will be one near you, find it, bring it and enter …

- Find your way up to the Firmament. At the top you may find yourself in another world, in the sky, in space, Sometimes you find yourself in or near a tower or castle or mountain or pyramid, don't have preconceptions. And there may be someone waiting for you or there may not. Sometimes we find ourselves alone here at first and have to find our way to the place we're supposed to be. It can be like finding your way through a maze.

- Say your purpose aloud. Say it three times.
"I am here to meet my Teacher

- Wait! Look around you. What is there? Are there any clues as to which way to go? Ask your Familiar – they are there to help you.

- When *your* Teacher comes you *will* know. There will be a sign - but ask them "Are *you my Teacher*?" You occasionally get more than one at the same time. They will probably tell you what's going on but keep asking questions until you are sure. You can ask *"Who are you?"* and *"Can you help me find my Teacher?"*. These are useful questions and, more importantly, useful practice for you in learning to ask lots of questions.

• Remember – the only stupid question is the one you DIDN'T ask!

• Take very careful note of everything which happens to you. Changes are particularly important. You may not understand them straight away but just store them up – you'll have your voice record on tape – and wait.

If you're told to go in a direction or to a place or with someone, go – after you have checked with your Familiar.

If you are given a gift, accept it– but if you feel any doubts check with your Familiar.

• You will know when the experience is over. You may well be "hustled" out, feeling that you've nearly overstayed your welcome! Don't worry. This is quite OK, remember your Teacher is busy! Thank them and leave.

• At the Call Back signal, or before if you're ready earlier, make your way back to your Beginning Place, your *known route home*. Don't forget to thank your Beginning Place.

• FIND YOURSELF BACK IN YOUR SACRED SPACE, *with your Familiar* – for goodness sake don't leave them behind, this is very bad etiquette! Spend some time recalling the experience, honouring it and assimilating within you. *When you are both ready*, return to your blanket and spend a couple of minutes lying on your side in the foetal position. Come back gently and quietly.

• CLOSE THE INTERFACE in which you've been working.

• FINALLY, CLEAR UP THE PLACE PHYSICALLY, dismantle your altar, put your candles, incense, water, stone away. Clean up any ash. Shake out your bedding, blanket and scarf and put them away. Mark up your tape with the day and subject and put it safe. Pack up all the *techyknowledgy* so the place is free of your journey.

• DRAW OR WRITE SOMETHING STRAIGHT AWAY as soon as you are back. Remember, the magical act of drawing or writing first impressions is very potent.

• LISTEN TO THE TAPE WITH YOUR FAMILIAR, witness yourself as you listen to the tape of your journey. When you have heard it right through, make drawings or notes. And write it up in your diary. Go over it again after a couple of days and see what new insights you get, always with your Familiar beside you. Don't forget, this is all good practice for conscious magical dreaming.

Note your feelings on listening to the tape again. Relate what is significant to your everyday life. A couple of days later listen to your journey again. Remember, it will bring up different things each time you listen. Don't forget to ask your Familiar for their comments, and your Teacher if they have any further comments or suggestions for you now you've listened to the tape again. Just note down what you are told, don't analyse.

Your Notes

Building your Dreamweb – The Centre

The centre will be about your Teacher and in some way be an image of them.

What do your Teacher and your Dreamweb want at the centre?

Again, OPEN THE INTERFACE, MAKE YOUR WORK-PLACE SACRED. Spread out your drawings and unwrap your Dreamweb, spread out the contents of your FINDS-BAG and begin your song again. It has probably grown since you began it, write down the new words in your diary on the dates when it grew. When you come to look back later you will be fascinated by the pattern you worked in.

As you sing you will find, as usual, that your hands do the selecting for you. It may be feathers, tassels, beads emblems, significant objects. The centre is the focusing point for you, the dreamer and for your Teacher, the Dream Maker. It will be the central lens through which you can communicate with each other.

The points around the rim of the Dreamweb are secondary focusing points. They are not stuck to being just one thing, but hold many significances at once. Allow them the full range.

Your Notes

Shapeshifting

Shapeshifting is one of the fundamentals of dreaming.

Blodeuwedd, the *Woman made from Flowers* one of the best known shapeshifters in the Celtic tradition. Gwydion and Math make her from the first spring growth of the Earth, the flowers of Spring, to be the wife of the Sun god, Llew Llaw Gyffes .

She is about rebirth, new growth, awakening. And it is through her apparent betrayal and the pain of death that the sun god comes to maturity. Before this he is a "boy", naive, selfish, autocratic and blind. Without falling in love with Blodeuwedd, who is also his sister, and having his childish belief system shattered by her he would never go on to be the god of summer harvest at his festival of Lughnasadh.

Llew shapeshifts too. As Gronw Pebyr's spear pierces him he does not die but is transformed through his uncle-father, Gwydion, into his totem, an eagle, a bird from his mother's realm of Mag Mell. Gwydion finds him and restores him to his human form with the aid of Ceridwen who shapeshifts into Hen Wen, the magical white sow.

All of this is about the way in which you are taught in your dreams. The Many Coloured Land is a good place for shapeshifting, you really do feel and see yourself in another shape. For most people this is an especially hard feat to accomplish in the relatively ordinary waking state or even on an ordinary journey. In dreams it happens quite naturally although sometimes it can be disconcerting and/or frightening. People often feel out of control when they find themselves in another shape but you can learn how to do this f your own volition with the help of your Familiar and your Teacher and the other Beings in Otherworld.

You probably recall times in your dreams where you "became" something or someone else, found yourself "looking out" through the eyes of someone else. This is classic shapeshifting and we all do it "by accident" in our dreams but to dream magically and consciously we need to learn how to do it at our own volition.

One contributor wrote –

… it is interesting these humanoid animal figures, I once came across some cat people in my dreamings. Also once I was given wolf/fox like ears to wear in a dream as a disguise. It is also interesting how we have a knack of denying some things in our everyday existence, and recognising them in our dreamings.

I once found what I can only describe as an elf in my dream as transparent as glass. I picked him up and fed him until he was more stronger. When I woke up I realised that I felt starved of creativity and that my academic commitments were preventing me from doing all the things that I wanted to do, dance, drum, drawing and making. I promptly took some time out and did a dance weekend and felt much better, Phew I thought, that was close.

The exercises you are going to do will help you to learn how to do this consciously so that you will find it easier to understand what happens in your dreams and be able to use it creatively. You become more focused. You will need to practice this exercise several times before you feel confident and competent enough to put it into practice in dreams, but that goes for all the exercises. Doing them only once will not get you to a reasonable state of competence. You need *time* to put all you learn into your "auto pilot", so you know automatically what to do and don't have to go look in the manual!

Your Notes

The following pages give several basic exercises which will help you to become competent in shapeshifting.

EXERCISE: TO EXPERIENCE SHAPESHIFTING

This is a breathing exercise and you will probably need to practice it a bit before it comes naturally. You are going to learn to breath like someone or something else.

First of all you need to learn how you breathe. We all do this on auto-pilot and consequently are not usually conscious of how we do it. Sit quietly now and just listen to yourself breathe. Don't worry, don't try to change anything, just listen.

Next, notice which parts of your body move as you breathe. It may be your shoulders, neck, stomach. Even legs and arms do move as we breathe. Feel you face. Is it stiff, loose, frowning? Look at yourself in a mirror and watch yourself breathe.

You will probably find that you want to change things a bit. Don't berate yourself just notice when you are not breathing as you would like and change to that state. As you practice you will find the habits gradually change. This is much better than shouting at yourself and feeling guilty! You will probably notice that the other exercises you are doing will change the way you breathe and consequently the way you feel.

Your Notes

EXERCISE: BREATHING WITH A FRIEND

How we breathe has so much to do with how we feel and think and consequently react. If you can find a friend who will be your model for the first time or two this will give you lots of helpful feedback. There is one possible drawback though – you both have to be completely honest! If you feel angry or jealous or mean while you are breathing like your friend you have to be able to say this to them and they have to be able to hear it, which is extremely difficult! If you are fortunate enough to have such a friend, treasure them. The purpose of this is so that you can explore what you feel and get real feedback from the friend.

- Watch the other person, note how they breathe. Which parts of the body are moving, shoulders, neck, ribs, hips, legs, arms? Does their face twitch? Is there a frown? Smile? Swallowing? Fingers trembling?

- Observe the person really closely.

- Listen to the sound their breathing makes.

- Listen to the rhythm of their breathing and watch the rhythm of the body movements.

As you watch try to copy the movement, breathing, rhythm, sound. You won't get it all at once but try each thing you notice on its own first. And, as you copy their breathing, sense into yourself, how does this make you feel? Make a note of this.

Sometimes it can feel very unpleasant to breath like someone else, probably because the person is in an uncomfortable state. If this happens, stop copying them straight away and take several deep slow breaths yourself. Stop looking at them too. Go into yourself Inner Sacred Space, ask your Familiar to help you clean up and refresh yourself. When you are ready, return to the everyday.

Don't forget, you can go into your Sacred Space anywhere and everywhere, in a café, office, bar, bus, washing up, in the bath, wherever. You might need it any time!

Your Notes

EXERCISE: CAFÉ PERSON BREATHING!

If you are a "café person" and do "people watching" this is a good place to practice. Once you get the hang of it you will be able to flick in and out again very quickly. If you are within hearing range in the café you can confirm your findings by eavesdropping – don't act shocked, we all do it!

Shapeshifting is about becoming someone or something else. This is a way of doing it which requires no unnerving physical changes which might shock the waiter into dropping your coffee. It also teaches you a way of removing yourself from being the other person by changing your breathing back to your own normal mode.

Keep notes in your diary of what you find when you do this. Watch how your entries change. Watch also how you change as you become more aware of breathing.

Your Notes

- EXERCISE: FOR WHEN YOU GO TO SLEEP

  - When you go to bed, lie quiet on your back as flat as you comfortably can.

  - Become aware of your breathing.

  - As you breathe IN sense, see, feel, the breath rising up out of the Earth, through you, through the soles of your feet, up your legs, hips, through your body, chest, shoulders, up your neck, up through your head and out of the top of your head up into the Heavens.

  - As you breathe OUT sense, see, feel, the breath flowing down through you, through the top of your head, down your neck, into your shoulders, chest, body, down through your hips, down your legs, into your feet and out through the soles of your feet into the Earth.

  - Feel the breath passing in from the Earth, through you and up to the Heavens.

  - Feel the breath passing out of the Heavens, through you and into the Earth.

  - After 5 breaths, STOP and come back to normal breathing. You are taking 5 breaths, one for each element and one for the soul.

This is an exchange process, where you are the physical bridge through which the breath-energy passes going between the worlds. You are physically the bridge between the worlds.

You will likely find this a very calming exercise which may help you to sleep better. It can be easy to "drift off" whilst doing this ... DON'T! It is important to stay conscious during the exercise otherwise you lose all benefit.

After the exercise turn on your side and curl up in the foetal position. Go to sleep!

Your Notes

EXERCISE: JOURNEY TO MEET THE SHAPESHIFTER

This journey will be to the realm of the ancestors and to the Guardian of the Beasts who is a master Shapeshifter. He (and it is a masculine energy) is able to become any beast in creation and, with the help of your Familiar,

- FIRST, PREPARE YOUR PHYSICAL SPACE as you will now be in the habit of doing

- SET UP YOUR ALTAR

- OPEN THE INTERFACE

- TURN ON THE TECHNOLOGY. When you are ready, lie down, *put your headphones on with the drumming tape.* Is your tape recorder on to record your journey …?!

- COVER YOUR EYES. Now, if you are comfortable, begin …

- FIND YOURSELF IN YOUR SACRED SPACE Spend a moment or two reacquainting yourself.

- Call your Familiar to you – if they are not already there. Say that you are going on an Lowerworld journey to meet the Shapeshifter and ask them to come with you, to help and guard and guide you. Be sure they agree this is the right time for you to do this. If they are adamant that you shouldn't go then follow their advice, however disappointed you may be. Remember, they know what they're doing and there will be another time. When you're BOTH ready, go out.

- FIND YOURSELF AT YOUR BEGINNING PLACE. Say aloud that you are on an Lowerworld Journey and would like to enter Otherworld. Give a gift if asked, remember there will be one near you, and then enter …

- Follow your Familiar DOWN, perhaps through tunnels, caves, tree roots, to the Lowerworld. At the bottom stop. Look about you, where are you, who is there? You may well find yourself in a cave, or a grove with the Great Horned One there beside his cauldron and all the beasts around him, like in the stories. But it may appear quite differently for you. Don't be worried, ask your Familiar to make sure.

- Say your purpose aloud. Say it three times.
"I am here to meet the Shapeshifter".

- WAIT! Something will happen.

- When the Shapeshifter appears, if he hasn't already, ASK *"Are you the Shapeshifter?* PLEASE, NEVER FORGET THIS.

- It is quite likely that the next few minutes will be very active. You have asked for experience and learning of shapeshifting and the Shapeshifter will take you at your word! You may find yourself suddenly "taken over" either inside something or with something inside you. If you are nervous call your Familiar and ask for help.

It's quite OK and very effective to shout "HELP!" – you always get it. And you don't have to remember obtuse ritual language, everyday-speak does just fine!

If you want things to slow down a bit, say so. If you want things to stop, say so. You do *not* have to submit to anything if you don't wish. However, if you can manage to ride your fears and go with it you will find the experience very rewarding. Just don't forget that "they", the Otherworld. Beings, are on your side in this, they are *not* out to get you.

- Changes are particularly important, as usual – keep talking out loud to the tape.

- When the experience is over you may well feel the "separation" as quite emotional, and for some people even physically painful.

YOU WILL STILL BE IN OTHERWORLD AS THE SHAPESHIFTER MOVES OUT OF YOUR SOUL-SPACE, DO NOT TRY TO COME BACK TO THE BLANKET TOO SOON.

It is an *extremely intimate* thing, to share consciousness another being. Even more than making love although there are similarities. Don't be afraid to cry, shiver, shake, swear, shout, scream, no-one in Otherworld will take offence! Ask your Familiar to help you.

- Spend a little time in Lowerworld, the Beings there will help you recover. You also have time to say thank you to those who have helped you. The Guardian of the Beasts may offer you a drink from his cauldron. Check with your own feelings and your Familiar that this is appropriate for you at this time. If it is, drink. Drinking here is a commitment to keeping and honouring your connection with the Otherworld

- At the Call Back signal, or before if you're ready, make your way back to your Beginning Place and thank it for helping you!

- Find yourself back in your Sacred Space WITH your Familiar.. Spend time recuperating, recalling the experience, honouring and assimilating it within you. *When you are both ready*, return to the blanket and spend a couple of minutes lying on your side in the foetal position. Come back gently and quietly. Honour what you've done and give it time.

- Close the Interface in which you've been working, as is your normal habit now.

- Finally, clear up the place physically, dismantle your altar. Put your candles, incense, water, stone, away. Clean up any ash. Pick up your bedding, blanket, scarf, shake them out and put them away. Take out your tape and mark it with the day and subject and put it safe. Pack up all the *"techyknowledgy"* so the place is free of your journey.

- Draw or write your first impressions after meeting the Shapeshifter as a potent magical act.

- Listen to the Tape – Witness yourself as you listen to the tape of your journey with your Familiar beside you. When you have heard it right through, make drawings or notes and write it up in your diary. Go over it again after a couple of days and see what new insights you get and ask your Familiar for their comments and insights now.

Your Notes

Pictures

Find books with pictures of Faerie, mythical and alchemical beasts and spend time just looking at them. Look in architectural and archaeological books. Faerie beings, such as the Green Man, the Sheelagh-na-gig and many others were carved in churches, pews, temples and houses all over the world.

There is a wealth of these carvings in British churches – perhaps the carvers were 5th columnists seeking to keep alive the old traditions despite the fervour of the new Christianity. Also, some early Christians tried to integrate the old with the new rather than just smash and suppress it. One subterfuge I like was told me by a Greek friend from Crete where the people were told to stop worshipping Ares and Poseidon so they did, officially. However they merely renamed Ares as St George and Poseidon as St Nicholas and carried on just the same!

When you go round old villages and churches in Britain look out for shapeshifting beasts. One of the most famous instances is in Winchester cathedral which has a host of Green Man figures carved in the choir. There are also many Pelicans pecking their breasts (an alchemical symbol) which was taken up by the founding bishop ... one wonders what he knew ... and lots of other animal and human figures seeming to grow one from the other.

All of this is about shapeshifting, of one thing assuming the guise of another. In carving these symbols into the fabric of the church the artists were also imbuing it with links and connections to Otherworld Making

You may want to draw, carve, make or craft your own shapeshifting igures, representations of the Beings you have shared consciousness with in your journeys. As with your Dreamweb, prepare your work-space, call the directions and open the Interface. Attune yourself to your Familiar and Teacher. Then allow your hands to lead you into the creation AND allow the creation to lead you into the shape it wishes to be. You are not working towards having an exhibition at the Tate Modern! This is for you and for Otherworld, it may be that you never show these works to anyone else. Remember, secret and sacred often go together. And don't forget to close the Interface and clear your space when you finish.

Your Notes

Building your Dreamweb – Shapeshifter

You are now going to build things into your Dreamweb which will symbolise and connect you with the Shapeshifter.

Again, call the directions and open the Interface making your work-place sacred. Spread out the drawings from your journey and unwrap your Dreamweb. Open your Finds-Bag and spread out the contents. Be still at first, no singing, chanting or anything. Ask your Familiar to be close to you. Gently recall the experience of shapeshifting.

You will probably find this to be a very "concentrated" piece of working, likely done in silence. But if a song, hum or chant comes to you don't reject it, allow it to sound through you as you work.

Never worry if the work is not completed in one session. Otherworld has its own ways of doing and being, it is not like a schoolteacher with a time for the homework to be in. You may find that you begin this piece of the work and that you don't have everything you need. It may come to you what thing, or things, are missing and you may also see how and where to find them or you may need to wait without knowing for some time. Perhaps you need to close down, pack up the making again and go straight out and get the things. If so, do that. Whatever, listen to your instincts and intuition and check them out with your Familiar.

Although this work is very much about using ritual it is *not* about getting stuck in the form of the ritual. You learn to be flexible while working within a form. Each ritual, each journey, each magical working and each dream are different from any before or after them. Just because you did so-and-so last time or took this long, doesn't mean you have to rigidly follow the same format this time. Everything in the universe, including you and your dreams, is changing and evolving all the time.

Your Notes

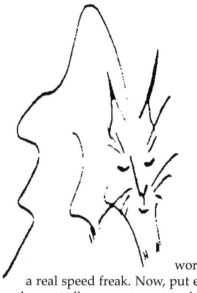

Day Dreaming

By this time you will have been working for some weeks, even if you are a real speed freak. Now, put everything aside for at least three days, then get all your notes out and look at them again from the beginning. Make a quiet time, turn the phone off, make yourself a pot of tea, put the "do not disturb" sign on the door.

OPEN THE INTERFACE AND MAKE YOUR SPACE SACRED. Pull all the notes out, spread them around on the floor. Begin to make patterns of them. Look for similarities.

One way of doing this is to get a very large piece of paper, wrapping paper, wall paper, kids drawing paper – but it must be plain, not lined – and put this on the floor. Then as you go through the notes start making groupings of words that stand out to you today – not one's you think ought to stand out but those that really do "ping" off the page at you. You may need to go through the notes more than once for this to start to happen. Can you see how these words might correlate?

WORDS	ELEMENTS
WORM, EARTH	**Earth** – and some air as blackbirds eat worms
BLACKBIRD, WING, FLURRY, FLIGHT, FEATHER, HOP	**Air** – and some earth with "hop"
SKY, FLASH, SUN	**Fire** – and some air perhaps as in a bird's "flashing" flight

No water is there? No matter, you don't always get all the elements but do you see what you are doing in drawing together images, how you begin building your own vocabulary of dream language? This is what you do in dream weaving, practise the skills of observation and correlation. Practical "day-dreaming is another step to conscious dreaming, get in touch with your imaginative faculties and learn how to use them.

Successful, creative dreaming is not really possible without a reasonably well tuned imagination and the ability to use it. When you begin to work with your imagination it is often very unruly, rather like the first time in the car. Remember driving lessons? When your feet haven't got a clue and you take off from the traffic light in a series of bounds like a kangaroo! After a few lessons your feet get the hang of it and you pull away smoothly. Learning to work with your imagination is the same sort of process.

If you speak and work with your feet, hands, body, lungs, etc., then you can begin to recognise they each have their own "life", and "intelligence". You can treat them with the same kindness you would a child, a cat or a dog. Where you would be harsh on *yourself*, critical, perfectionist, you can allow your hands some slack. They have their own individuality *as well as* being part of your body.

Go back and do the exercise in befriending the four subtle bodies again. Hopefully you have been doing this every week anyway but if not begin again now. It is very important to know your personality body (which is made up of the four subtle bodies) well and have a good, equal, working relationship with it. It is the container for your soul and if it fails you your soul will have no-where to complete its incarnation. You will die – and without having completed all the plans you carefully made for this lifetime. Seems a bit of a waste … ???

Try to make it a regular thing, at least once a week, to check in with your four subtle bodies through this exercise. You really will find it beneficial, provided you are willing to listen to what they tell you. This is often the problem area for people – the subtle bodies are not tactful and rarely say what we would like to hear!

Your Notes

Building your Dreamweb – Pathways

Weavers, such as the Celts, Navajo and Greeks, made '*paths* leading out of the weaving pattern in their rugs and blankets. The old 'traders' used to think these were 'mistakes' so the weavers learned to hide the paths to get the best deal from the traders. You are going to build paths into your Dreamweb. You use these paths to help you to find your way in and out of the Interface and between the Many Coloured Land your everyday reality.

Some people use plaited or knotted threads which hang down from the centre as a *path out* which you can follow back to waking life. Others use feathers or weave a different coloured wool across the web in places. Some people make a path through the web with feathers, bones or twigs. You may want to use twigs or pieces of bone or patterns of beads or leaves across the web or hanging from it. If your Dreamweb is a piece of material with things attached to it you might want to paint pathways onto the material.

Again, OPEN THE INTERFACE and make your work-place sacred. Make sure your Familiar is with you. Take out the drawings from your day-dreaming sessions, unwrap your Dreamweb, open your FINDS-BAG and spread out the contents. Begin your song again if it wishes to come and don't forget to write down the new words in your diary.

Allow your hands to lead you in building the paths. If you feel "stuck" ask your Familiar for help and also ask the Dreamweb itself what it wants. Again, don't have preconceptions about what is "correct", there's no such thing from outside yourself and your relationship with Otherworld. You are not making this for anyone else's approval.

When you have finished, CLOSE THE INTERFACE AGAIN, clear your space and wrap everything so that it is held together and away from other eyes, keep it sacred and secret.

Your Notes

Dedicating your Dreamweb

You will need to dedicate your Dreamweb. It may not be finished, in a sense it never will be, but it should now be in a place where it feels whole enough to be used and at this point you will need to make a *formal* journey to meet its spirit and agree to work together.

Prepare the physical space carefully and bring your Dreamweb into it. Ask. Dreamweb in which direction it wishes to sit/stand/hang, then prepare the rest of the space to suit while all the time checking back with Dreamweb that you have things right.

Ask Dreamweb how it would like you to be – sitting, lying, standing. Ask if you are likely to have to move about during the ritual. The ritual will very likely "grow" as you are actually doing it and I cannot give you a formula as it will all depend on you and your Dreamweb. You cannot force the thing into a set structure and it is quite wrong to try. Check out if you need rattles, drums, bells, or any other instruments, what incense (if any) you should use, candles, water, vessels, stones and/or earth. It is worth while you insisting that you need to have representatives of the four elements although it is very unlikely Dreamweb will object.

Some people find their Dreamweb wishes to be "processed", i.e. carried in ritual procession, around the four/eight directions either widdershins or deosil, or maybe in both directions. Allow yourself to say the words you need to say rather than making up some highfalutin sounding ritual before hand. Most people find that, if they allow themselves, they say the most meaningful things which are very pertinent to them at that particular time.

As this is an *initiatory* process I suggest you do *not* tape it. It is not meant to be repeated, you are only going to be able to experience this once. Each initiation changes you and everything around you – you cannot put the same genie back in the bottle again!

Use the basic process you have already learned, preparing the physical space, opening the Interface, doing the ritual, closing the Interface and clearing the physical space.

The Interface is the place where you work each night in dreams so it is good to have your Dreamweb hanging somewhere in the room where you sleep. This means you are both in close physical proximity all night and will find it easier to work together.

If you sleep with a partner you must be sure that it's OK to have your Dreamweb in the same room with them – both for the partner *and* the Dreamweb! And, if you have cats, you will need to convince them that you have not just made them a lovely new kitty toy! You can actually ask your Dreamweb to help with this by suggesting it sets up a sort of "force field" around itself which keeps unwanted paws and fingers out of the way without damage.

RITUAL TO MEET THE SPIRIT OF YOUR DREAMWEB

As part of dedicating your Dreamweb you need to journey to meet the spirit who is informing it, en-wholing it. Use the following ritual to do so.

- Prepare your sacred space and set up your altar as agreed with your Dreamweb.

- Open the Interface

- SAY YOUR PURPOSE OUT LOUD, 3 TIMES.
"I am here to meet the spirit of my Dreamweb".

- FIND YOURSELF IN YOUR SACRED SPACE. Spend a moment or two reacquainting yourself with it. Be at home with your Familiar beside you

- FIND YOURSELF AT YOUR BEGINNING PLACE. Say that you are on a Journey to meet the spirit of your Dreamweb and wish to enter.

- SAY YOUR PURPOSE ALOUD. "I am here to meet the spirit of my Dreamweb" 3 times. Now wait! Allow yourself to know what the next thing is to do.

- You will know when the spirit of your Dreamweb approaches but still ASK – never forget this rule wherever you are.

- Spend time with the spirit and go with them wherever they wish to take you. Also you may have a particular place which is intimate and special to you, say you would like to take the spirit of your Dreamweb there and show them. This kind of sharing will greatly enhance your relationship.

- You should also introduce the Spirit of the Dreamweb to your Familiar – they may already know each other but the formal introduction is very important too

- When you have all done all you need to do make your way back to your BEGINNING PLACE and remember to thank your beginning place for helping you! Invite the spirit of your Dreamweb to return to the everyday world with you.

- FIND YOURSELF BACK IN YOUR SACRED SPACE. Spend a little time recalling, honouring and assimilating the experience. Then return your consciousness fully to the room and spend a couple of minutes in contemplation.

- When you are back, you will know there is some final physical ritual which you will need to do, words to be said, special action to be done. Before you do anything else do this.

- Close your ritual AND THE INTERFACE in the usual way and dismantle your altar.

After the ritual it is important to spend some quiet time alone, with your Dreamweb and your Familiar, in the everyday space. You have just done some very big work, you need to assimilate it. Do not tell people about your ritual, or even that you have done it. You have nothing to prove to anyone and to talk of such a thing dissipates the energy and lessens the whole thing. It loses respect.

Your Notes

Using Your Dreamweb

The Dreamweb is your physical representation of the Interface, the place where the worlds meet. The Saxons used the word Wyrd to describe this. It seems to have been the idea of a web, like a spider's web and the spider is one of the archetypal images for the Sun, the creator-spirit, in many traditions around the world. Your Dreamweb is like a tiny representation of this cosmic web, this Wyrd. The Many Coloured Land, the dream world, contains all the possibilities of human consciousness *and* that of animals, plants, planets, stars, galaxies Dreamwebs are patterns, pattern holders and pattern shapers. They can be the *Threshold Guardian* who holds the dream until you are ready to work with it. They help you *incubate* dreams and bring them to fruition. They stop you being over-eager and damaging Otherworld by entering places when you are not yet ready. They are *Sacred Mirrors* in which you can see yourself truly – if you wish, a *Window to the Soul,* the part of you which continues across worlds and incarnations, and a *Gateway* enabling you to become a *Walker Between the Worlds..*

In C. S. Lewis Narnia story *The Magician's Nephew* they travel between worlds by mean of magical rings. You put on one colour ring and as soon as you do you find yourself in *The Wood Between the Worlds.* The wood is very green and soft and peaceful, it seems to be humming to itself. All the trees look alike and there are small pools as far as you can see between the trees which all look just the same too. It is a sleepy, dreamy place where you forget who you are, where you are, why you are there, you believe you have always been there. You have to know that this is going to happen to you and really concentrate so that you stay focused and are able to travel on into another world and return home again.

In the story, when you arrive in *The Wood Between the Worlds* you change rings to the other colour and then jump into one of the pools to go somewhere else. And here is another difficulty. All the pools look alike. There may be several around you. Which one was it you came out of, from your own world? Which one will take you back home? In the story the children mark the home-pool as soon as they realise their danger, that they might never find the right pool to go home through. They also mark the other pools that they jump into to journey to other worlds so that they can distinguish between them and know where they are going.

The magician, the uncle, is not very competent and doesn't really understand what he has made in the rings, he gets into lots of difficulties through this which is part of the story. The children learn what the rings are about through using them.

Your Dreamweb is rather like the rings. It is your means of transporting yourself between worlds. But you have to know where you are and what it is doing or you will get lost too. The exercises you have been doing are to help you know your way around and understand the process. It all takes time. You cannot expect to know everything about it in just a few days or weeks, it takes most people several lifetimes at least!

The *Wood Between the Worlds* is like the Interface but by learning and working consciously with it you are able stay focused and remember where you are and why you came and how to get to where you want to go *and* home again. Until they learn focused, magical dreaming people are like the children are when they first find themselves in the *Wood Between the Worlds*, sleepy, dreamy, forgetful. They go to other worlds by accident and when they wake they don't know where they've been or what it was all about.

Because you built your Dreamweb consciously and through journeying you know it and it knows you. You built it piece by piece as you explored the Many Coloured Land and the friends you made there. It is your talisman, link, key, which helps you walk between the worlds *and* hold the Interface where the two worlds meet which is where you work.

Your Notes

Exercise: Using your Dreamweb

- Before trying this as you go to sleep practice with your Dreamweb in a waking state.

- Do your preparation, open the Interface and ask your Familiar to be with you. Then hold your Dreamweb in your vision physically. Later you will be able to imagine it with your eyes shut but don't expect to do so straight away.

- Follow one of the pathways from the outside in towards the centre, asking for a dream in which you will be active and working. When you reach the centre shut your eyes and rest there for a little while.

- When you wish to return out of the dream see one of the pathways going out from the centre towards the edge and follow it.

- Open your eyes again for this at first so you can physically see the path home.

- When you feel fairly practised and more confident do your normal before sleep invocation and then do this exercise.

- When you arrive at the centre allow yourself to go to sleep.

- It may take time and practice before you will find yourself naturally in the dream and at the centre of your Dreamweb, in the Interface working. Persevere.

- Ask to find one of the paths home at the end of your dream work, ask your Familiar to help you with this, and follow it home.

Again the journey home may take time and practice before you do it smoothly every time. Don't worry, this happens for all of us. Keep trying. Don't be disappointed when you don't succeed. You will.

Your Notes

EXERCISE: USING YOUR DREAMWEB AS A GATEWAY

Prepare your sleeping place. Open the Interface.

• As you go to sleep see your Dreamweb in front of you getting bigger and bigger. Feel yourself moving towards it as though it is a doorway or window or threshold – which, of course, it is. Be very focused and conscious as you pass through.

• As you arrive within the Interface, stop. Be still there. Sense into the place and call the directions – they do exist across time and space for they are the framework, the skeleton, on which all the worlds are built. They are the warp on which the weft of the worlds is woven. Our lives, our dreams, and those of every other living thing, are the weft.

• Move on into your dream.

• When you are ready, find yourself back within the Interface again. Draw in the threads of the web, the directions, fold the Interface up, putting it back into the "cosmic potential.

• See your Dreamweb in front of you again and very consciously pass back across the threshold into your sleep, your bed, the everyday world.

• When you are ready, awake and note the work you have done.

• Close your sleeping place and close the Interface again.

Your Notes

Dreaming

Preparation for Dreaming

Here is an invocation to do as you go to sleep each night.
North, East, South, West, Above, Below, Within,
Guide me, guard me, keep me
As I sleep and in the work I do
As I journey in the Many Coloured Land this night.
Bring me to new realisation in the morning.

And in the morning, when you wake up use this one
North, East, South, West, Above, Below, Within
Thank you for guiding, guarding and keeping me
As I slept last night and in the work I did
As I journeyed in the Many Coloured Land.
Bring me to new realisation this morning.

Spend a moment after you've said your morning invocation just to see what images and thoughts come into your mind. Draw or note them down, just as they come in your Dream Journal, then get up and go about the day. You may well get additional images and thoughts come to you through the day, if you are able to keep your Dream Journal with you note these down in it as soon as you can.

You should be reasonably practised by now at walking between the worlds and so there are likely to be a few images most mornings. None of us manages to have images every day but at least note the fact that you didn't in your Journal. Give yourself two or three weeks to establish this ritual of morning and evening invocations, or longer if you feel you need it – there is no "right" length of time to have done this by.

Keeping a Dream Journal

A dream journal is like a diary but allows you more freedom than the average diary. You should be able to draw in it as well as write, paint, stick things in it, like you do in your magical diary but it will be a bit more specific than that. Plain rather than ruled pages are better for drawing and give you permission to write all over the place rather than in neat rows. This helps you dream better. Dreams are *not* neat!

You want to record –	the date *and* the day of the week
	Moon cycle dark, waxing, full, waning
	the moon's astrological sign
	astrological sign of the Sun

There are diaries with this information already printed in them, so you know where you are cosmically as well as planetarily.

If you have nothing to write up the dates will still be held and you will see when you look back over the journal in later years that there was a "gap" of however long in places. This helps you see patterns. Even if you have no dream to report it is worth noting briefly what was going on in your life anyway, this may show you why you have no remembered dreams at that time.

Don't try to give a blow by blow account with all the details. A set of "clues" which will re-evoke the dream in your mind when you come to read them again is far more useful. Don't try to write good grammar – dreams don't do good grammar and if you try to translate them into it you will lose 80% of the "reality" of the dream – see this extract from my own journal.

Running. Madly. Up hill. Path falls away under each step but still I run. Top. Breathless. Rain streams down. Light over head – moon, searchlight, don't know. Is it light or rain streaming over me? Snake-tower opens hood and rattles at me. I hiss back. I'm bigger than it now. I bite its head off, swallow. Scales scratch my throat.

I also had a drawing of the tower and me, just a kid's scribble type of thing, but it reminds me which side I was when I got to the top by the tower, I don't say in the note. I used crayons to draw it and this reminds me of the colours, the rain-light was pale yellow-gold, the sky very dark, night and I drew myself in red which was significant at the time.

As you practice keeping your dream journal you will find your own style develop which is most meaningful to you. You will have your own "short-hand" for things. You can also cross-refer dream to dream which will be very revealing. Many people get "series" dreams, soap-opera continuations, with your journal notes you will see how the whole story unfolds and how it interacts with and tells you about things in your everyday life. You will begin to understand the language in which your dreams speak to you. This is not like going to a foreign language class. Everybody does not speak "dream-language" the same way, we each do it differently and your way is at least as good as mine!

People say they have difficulty remembering anything when they wake up and so can't keep a dream journal. This is often because the transition from dream to waking is very abrupt. If you have to use an alarm of some kind so that you get up on time try to use one such as the radio coming on with some gentle music rather than a frenetic clanging and screeching bell!

Don't move – when you very first wake up. Keep still, don't open your eyes, don't try to think. Your body-sensations may be able to help you remember where you have just been, feel into them, where are the relaxed bits, do you have that wonderful warm-can't-move sensation? Sense the pillow, the feel of the cotton. Now, very gently, ask your body to show you where you were in the dream.

Many people find this gentle, careful, awakening brings the whole dream back quite quickly. Again, don't move. Don't sit up and try to write it out straight away. Go over the dream in your own mind. Remind yourself of particular words, colours, sensations, feelings. If you have time when you finish the first time through go over it again, still without moving. Then you can sit up gently and begin your drawings and notes.

If you live with your family then you must also educate them as to what you are doing. Even if they think you are "really weird" tell them this is what you need to do and will they please respect it and give you your space. It's very hard to learn this work if you get bounced or pounced as soon as you wake up! Negotiate a space between waking and getting together with the rest of the family – you have to include the cats and dogs in this too! But you also need to make sure they know they will have some of your time too and that you are not deserting them for your magical work. It is not more important than your family – they are all part of the same thing, this is what you are learning.

Also, do not try to teach what you are learning to your poor unsuspecting family! They may not wish to do it and you must leave them space to choose for themselves, not proselytise or coerce! As to your cats and dogs – they are already past masters and certainly don't need your help – just watch any cat doing catnappery – however they may well be willing to offer you their help and become your Familiar.

Conscious Dreaming

Get confident with your night and morning invocations, your breathing practice and recording the images and journeys which come each night. Allow time for the Many Coloured Land, to teach you about dreaming now that you have some tools to use and friends to go with. You have used particular processes to journey, to find your sacred space, your beginning place, you Familiar and your Teacher, You have had some experience with the Shapeshifter, the Dream-Master, Continue your practice in journeying and gradually build it into dreaming.

Remember – ask questions in dreams just as you do in journeys. Ask your Familiar to be with you each night and dream together. They can then help you remember in the morning. If/when you find yourself in a "nightmare yell out for your Familiar to help you! Remember, you are no longer alone. As you journey more you will gain friends in Otherworld and you can also call on them to come to you and help you in your dreams.

You are getting to know new worlds and their inhabitants as well as the terrain, and they are getting to know you. In your dream journal try keeping the following questions as a guide for recall.

How   Where   When   What   Who

You don't have to answer them in that order, in fact which one you answer first may change with each time you do it.

Notice the "why" question isn't there. That's because answering the other five questions will give yoo the answer to "why". If you begin with "why" you'll stay in your head and play mind games rather than finding out what really is there.

These questions help you "organise" your initial images. Don't use them first! Continue to put down the disorganised images just as they come to you in your first half-waking stillness. Then, later, maybe in the evening or over lunch, look over the images again and try sitting them beside each of these questions. You can use the same techniques as you do with Day Dreaming, drawing and writing on a large sheet of paper and grouping the images. See what dream-patterns emerge and how they relate to your everyday life at that time.

Your Notes

Re-entering a dream while awake

- Prepare your sacred space and turn on the *techyknowledgy*.

- SIT UP IN A CHAIR – this is not a time to lie down as you will need your consciousness to be readily available to you.

- Call your Familiar to you and read together through the notes of the dream you wish to re-enter. Your Familiar can help you a lot with this so don't leave them out.

- State your purpose out loud, 3 times

- "I wish to re-enter the dream I had last whenever…"

- Now, go to the beginning of your dream and take yourself through it to the point where it stopped, then ask to go forward. Say something like *"I wish to go forward in this dream"*. If you feel resistance or difficulty ask your Familiar to help you go through this.

- If there is any reason why you should not do this at the moment your Familiar will advise you. This is unlikely though as your Familiar would most likely have said before you began the process. However, if you are told to stop, do so.

- As you find your way forward into the next part of the dream keep talking out loud to the tape. You will want to know everything that happens and this is the easiest way. I always use a 90 minute tape so I have a full 45 minutes per side however, occasionally, this has been known to run out and I have had to turn the tape over in the middle of the session. This is why I suggested you sit up. You will hear the tape stop. You can ask your Familiar and anyone else present to "hold" for a moment while you turn the tape over and then resume the dream. It is very good for you to learn to work in two worlds at once in this way and without losing anything.

- You may find that the dream "comes to the end of a chapter" and that you can only go so far. This is fine. Everyone has "serial dreams" and it is very exciting to wait for the next episode. Most people's dreams are definitely better than "soaps"!

- When you have come to the stopping point for this session bring yourself back to the chair and spend a moment becoming conscious of your everyday body again – and thanking it for still being there for you to return to!

- Spend time with your Familiar ask them for their thoughts, views, opinions and recording these onto the tape. Thank them for being with you and helping.

- Turn off the *techyknowledgy* and close your sacred space.

- LISTEN TO THE TAPE *straight away* and make any notes about the continuation of the dream into your dream journal. Mark the tape and keep it so that you can refer back. If it was a "to be continued" dream you may want to use the other side for the next episode.

- RELATE THE DREAM to things that are happening in your life, questions you are asking, advice you need.

Dreams are not "instant tea" they require us NOT to write things off just because we don't understand them. It is not the dreams which are screwed up but our own inner attitudes which need expanding to include more reality! If you do not understand something then you ask for help with it, from your Familiar and your Teacher. Tell them you do not understand, ask them to show/tell you again, perhaps in a different way, or to put an event into your life which will make it more obvious to you. We all get cross sometimes and have a bit of a shouting match with our Familiars and even our Teachers – this is OK, but do expect them to shout back!

Your Notes

Structure

After some months, when you have a good bit of experience recording your dreams and beginning to find their patterns, you may want to add in a bit of structure. Perhaps you wish to find the answer to a question through dreams. Remember how you structure your journeys, you have a specific purpose in mind and you state it out loud at the beginning. You can use a variation of this for dreaming.

As well as saying your purpose out loud, write it down and put it under your pillow. When you do your invocation before sleeping ask your Familiar to be with you and to help you have the appropriate experiences in your dream to lead you to the answer you need.

Now that phrasing was deliberate and important. We do not control dreams or outcomes, we don't make childish or arrogant assumptions that we "know what's best" or that we can have anything we want. If you have a problem you don't know how to work with, ask your Familiar to help you phrase a question which *allows* the APPROPRIATE outcome to the problem for you *and* for all the rest of the world! Remember – you are not separate from everything else in this world and Otherworld, Everything that happens to you affects everything in all the worlds. Yes I know, that sounds horrendously big but even physics would agree!

To dream consciously is to become aware of the interconnections of everything – including you! You have been experiencing that in the journeys you've made and now the dreams you have. So, if you want help you have to learn to ask for it in a way which allows outcomes you've not yet dreamed of to happen!

The basic principles are –

- State the problem – succinctly

- Ask to be shown the *appropriate outcome* in the dream.

Sometimes (often!) we get the question wrong so the dream shows us this rather than giving us an answer. Until we get experienced we tend to ask for selfish outcomes and to blame people – e.g. *"How can I teach Fred a lesson for hurting me?"*. The answer from the dream here is likely to show you your own culpability – very uncomfortable!

A more appropriate question might be *"How can I sort out this trouble I am having with Fred so that I stop feeling so hurt/angry/vengeful/murderous?"*. This question would probably bring you some novel ideas for solutions. They would likely be reasonably painless too, for you, Fred and everyone else. Are you getting the idea?

When you get used to this sort of working you will find yourself more competent at asking supplementary questions whilst you are within the dream which will enable it to change its structure. So if you are not getting the point you can say so and things will change to offer you another way of seeing it. Once you've got the hang of this, keep on asking until you've got the message from the dream. This is another reason why you learn to ask questions all the time!

Practice makes perfect – but really "perfect" never comes as there's always more to learn and know. Keep on practising anyway so that your horizons and your whole self become larger and more inclusive all the time. As long as there's always more to know it stays exciting to go to bed and dream! If you use the basic techniques you've learned in this book and allow the Many Coloured Land to build on them and teach you more, your dream life will expand and expand all the days of your life. And so will your everyday life. Each feeds the other, your consciousness grows and you find life more and more fun.

Do try it!

Your Notes

The Many Coloured Land

This is the land of dreams itself. Like in a journey, you learn to recognise where you are through feel, smell, touch, taste or hearing as much as sight, to *know* which world you are in, Upper or Lower or Middleworld, as an overall guide. Sometimes the dream may encompass all the three major worlds. When you are beginning with conscious dreaming it is better to get used to working in one world at a time first and learning to do this teaches you how to interact and choose while within the dream. The three main spheres are –

- *Lowerworld* – place of Ancestors, where all *knowing* is stored;

- *Upperworld* – place of Powers, where all *potential* is;

- *Middleworld* – spiritual counterpart of the everyday world, where things change. It feeds both upper and lower worlds.

The Many Coloured Land has specific places which are always there – somewhere – but there is a lot of room for you to find, create, discover places which are your own. This is part of your creative work in Otherworld – to expand *its* boundaries.

The Many Coloured Land

Arianrhod's
Castle

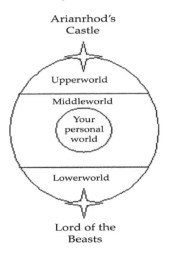

Lord of the
Beasts

This diagram looks very similar to the psychological map known as **Assagioli's Egg**, created by the transpersonal psychologist Roberto Assagioli.

It is similar but the main difference is that Assagioli used it to help map inner consciousness and I am using it here as a plan of the Many Coloured Land, which exists beyond and in its own right apart from personal inner consciousness. This is an important distinction, as has already been said, that the dream world exists apart from humanity and *not* because of it.

The Hazelnut

The **Hazelnut** is one of the major images for the universe in Celtic tradition. Within it is the Great Tree of Wisdom and Tradition whose roots wrap around the lip of the Well of Segais, the fountain of all knowledge and wisdom.

By the well sits the Lord of the Beasts guarding the Cauldron of Rebirth and around him are the Beasts and the Ancestors. Sometimes it appears like a great hall, sometimes a grove. It may be daylight, twilight or night. This is the Lowerworld, lit by the Earth stars, the crystals.

The Tree of Wisdom and Tradition reaches its branches up into the heavens and beyond. They are full of stars and the Sun and Moon hang among the branches. This is the Upperworld, the realm of Arianrhod, Lady of the Stars and Moon, Mag Mell, Caer Sidi.

Around the centre of the trunk of the Great Tree is Middleworld,, where we live out our earthly incarnations. It is the spiritual dimension of the everyday world, holding the essences, the blueprints, of everything in our daily lives.

Surrounding the Hazelnut is the Rainbow. This great band of colour defines our universe from others. This is the Rainbow which is the Bridge, the way to walk between the worlds - see the front cover of this book.

Within each of these worlds are "archetypal places such as the Well of Segais, the Mound of Wonders, Arianrhod's Spinning Tower, Arawn's castle, Annwn.

Then there is also a myriad of smaller places, often personal to the dreamer, and maybe having a counterpart in the everyday world. All of these will become familiar so you know your way *there and back again*, as Bilbo said.

You have already visited Lowerworld, where you met your Familiar, and Upperworld where you met your Teacher. You live in the physical counterpart of Middleworld and are getting to know its spiritual counterpart, the first parts of which are your Sacred Space and your Beginning Place.

Dreams take you to all of these places, sometimes all within the same dream and sometimes a dream goes to one specific realm.

Your Notes

EXERCISE: LOWERWORLD FAMILIARISATION

The following exercises will help you learn your way around.

Do your usual preparation and open the Interface.

- Turn on the *techyknowledgy*.

- SAY YOUR PURPOSE OUT LOUD, 3 TIMES.
"I am here to learn my way around Lowerworld.

- FIND YOURSELF IN YOUR SACRED SPACE. Spend a moment or two reacquainting yourself with it. Be at home with your Familiar beside you. When you're BOTH ready, go out ...

- FIND YOURSELF AT YOUR BEGINNING PLACE Say that you are on a Lowerworld Journey and would like to enter. If you are asked for a gift, find it, bring it and enter ...

- SAY YOUR PURPOSE AGAIN, ALOUD, 3 TIMES. " *I am here to learn my way around Lowerworld* ". Follow your Familiar DOWN to the Lowerworld, they will lead you. There may be someone waiting for you at the bottom or maybe not, don't have preconceptions. Keep following your Familiar and talking to them, ask questions about what you see.
Remember – the only stupid question is the one you DIDN'T ask!

- Take very careful note of everything which happens to you. Keep talking aloud so you have your voice record on tape.

- You may well be taken on a "there and back again" journey, or perhaps a circular one. When you find yourself back again where the journey began say thank you and leave.

- At the Call Back signal, or before if you are ready, make your way back to your Beginning Place. You should have a strong *known route home* by now but still thank it for helping you!

- FIND YOURSELF BACK IN YOUR SACRED SPACE, with your Familiar. Honour the experience, give it time. Recall and assimilate it, then spend a couple of minutes lying on your side in the foetal position before returning your consciousness to the room.

When you are back, sit up gently and *draw* your journey. This gives you a first map of Lowerworld. Don't worry if it doesn't seem like other descriptions you've read or been told of. Remember, *your* vision, view, perspective, of the worlds is unique to you – although it will probably share some features with other people's descriptions.

Don't forget to close the Interface and clear your space.

Your Notes

Thoughts and Ideas on Lowerworld

Lowerworld is under the charge of Arawn and Rhiannon and is called Annwn in the Welsh. The story of Pwyll in the Mabinogion gives a lot of information on this world. It is a prime source of wisdom and knowledge. It also holds your power until you are able to take it and use it without damaging everything around you. Your early conscious dreams to the Lowerworld will probably be about you taking on the responsibility of holding and using your own power in the everyday as well as the dream worlds.

As well as Rhiannon you will also find the Maiden and the Crone aspects of the goddess in the Lowerworld. The maiden aspect is often represented by Blodeuwedd, the woman made from flowers as the wife of the sun god, Llew Llaw Gyffes. His name means "lion of the clever hand". It is worth reading her story and spending a lot of time pondering on it. Like all the old tales it is not as simple as it first appears, there is no simple good and bad, right and wrong. You must also realise that you cannot put modern politically correct attitudes onto it either. Blodeuwedd is *not* a "victim" being used by "males", she is a power in her own right fulfilling a destiny and need of the Earth herself.

Blodeuwedd is a major "dream guide" because of the "geas" which she has undertaken – a geas is a duty or obligation *freely and willingly* entered into and agreed to by the one on whom it falls. The eastern traditions might call it "dharma. All of these Beings work together to make and re-make the patterns of the Web, the Wyrd, which are the worlds in which we live. As we learn to dream consciously so we take our part in this pattern-building too. Blodeuwedd in her owl-form is a guide and guardian to the dream world.

Another form of the Maiden is Creiddylad whose story is embedded within that of Culhwch and Olwen. The champions of summer and winter battle to win her favour and her hand in marriage. The same story is told over and over in Guinevere, Isolda, Maid Marian, and others.

Ceridwen is perhaps the best known name of the Crone aspect of the goddess. She is the Lady of the Cauldron, of death and rebirth, and her season comes in the five fallow days at the end of October which are a time between the end of one year and the beginning of the next in the Celtic cycle. Her name may come from the word *cyrrid* meaning hooked or crooked, and *benyw* meaning woman. She is the Creator/Destroyer aspect of the goddess, making life and death which are the same thing. She keeps the Cauldron of Inspiration, read the story of Taliesin for this, which is the way of knowing that "you *are* everything", not separate and apart from but a part of all the life with which you share this planet. Even in everyday physical terms this is true in that the atoms which make up your skin have been earth, rock, other animals, plants, water, etc and will be again when your body no longer needs them. Ceridwen adds in the non-ordinary reality side of this. She can be unnerving to meet, a joker and only too ready to make you jump out of your skin – which is part of her function. Try to be scared without fearing her … this is truly a vital part of the work, learning to be afraid successfully.

Other aspects of the Crone are Morgan le Fay, the Morrigan,, the Washer at the Fords, and many others. The witches in Faerie stories are versions of this, read them again and see what new ideas about them come to you now. Good/ bad, black/white, are not the simple things they are for those who live in the relatively small world of the non-conscious dreamer.

Although it is often called Lowerworld an old spelling of the Welsh name "Annwfn" can be translated as meaning "in-world", that which lies deep within at the heart, core or centre of everything. In this sense it is the source, the primal place from which all else stems.

All the worlds have "threshold guardians" who will test you before allowing you to enter or continue on your journey and they can appear in all sorts of guises. CG Jung used to say that the Unconscious (perhaps another way of seeing the Lowerworld contained your dragons who guard your treasure for you until you are able to use it wisely. And they challenge you – to make sure! Your Familiar will be able to help you in how to deal with such challenges and will also tell you if they don't think you are yet up for it! Don't get offended – they really do know best! You may find yourself having to "kill" a beautiful dragon in a dream who you would much rather make friends with. Be brave, do the deed, and watch what happens after. There is usually a wondrous transformation which is like an initiatory experience and will show you so much more of how magical dreaming works.

Ask your Familiar about this type of experience. They probably won't tell you much until after you have had it – any more than I am! – so don't go into the experience thinking you know what is going on. If you do then you won't learn much because you will be saying *"Oh yes! I understand. I know what's happening here"* and consequently you will miss all things the experience is trying to show you, blinding yourself, only wishing to believe what you *already* know.

Many people who work with the northern European traditions find a Tree to be one of the main features which recurs in their dream work. This might be Yggdrasil, the world tree of the Nordic traditions or the Tree of Wisdom and Tradition from Britain. It contains all the worlds which grow out from it so, in a sense, it is not just a Lowerworld thing however it is very often seen in Lowerworld dreams.

The idea of the central pole is common in all traditions throughout the world representing the idea of the Spindle which connects heaven and earth through the Middleworlds, the Axis Mundi. Circular dwellings with a central supporting pole and the circular mounds common in the Celtic lands are other representations of this.

The Tree also appears as the "Green and Burning Tree" This can seem very strange at first, one half of it is in full leaf and flower and fruit while the other is continuously consumed by fire but never burned up. The old Biblical story of Moses, the burning bush may well have come from a version of this.

This tree is about inspiration, Awen, as it is called in Welsh. The fire aspect is the "fire of heaven" which inspires us and the green aspect is how we can make it real in the world around us. The goddess Brighid or Britannia is the guardian of the Fires and so may well be someone you meet when you come to this tree. It is very much about the ability to be more than one thing at once – in this case both green and burning at the same time. Things which one might say were impossible to have together. Again, this is what magical dreaming is about, the ability to be, see, do, two things which your everyday mind would tell you were impossible to have together.

 The Green and Burning Tree often warns you to be on your guard in the sense of balancing, like a tightrope. A misplaced step and you could find yourself getting burned. It is about taking care of all the little details, another very important part of magical work which you have probably already realised. You cannot be slipshod in here, you must take care. It is one of the reasons why many people do not wish to be bothered with it!

Another common archetypal feature is a Mound, like Silbury Hill or Weyland's Smithy. If you can, visit these or similar places like tumuli and fougou. Go inside them, sit quietly by yourself. You will get extra experience which will help you when you dream.

Many people find the Enchanted Forest here in Lowerworld, Broceliande of the Arthurian stories and the forest where Merlin's Tower or castle is. It is, a place which changes its shape and moves about from place to place within the forest. The forest is alive, it is a being in its own right and its guardian is sometimes called the Woodward, Woodwose, Green Man, Lord of the Beasts, Custennin, from the tale of Culhwch and Olwen, and many other names.

Don't be surprised if you find places move from where you thought they were last time you visited Lowerworld, this is a normal and natural part of magical work. From our everyday perspective we tend to believe that places stay still, have their "feet nailed to the perch" as Monty Python put it! This is not really true in any sense for places grow and evolve of themselves, they are alive and have their own consciousness. It is sometimes easier for humans to believe that things are small enough to be under their control but this is an illusion brought on by the absence of magical experience. Magicians control nothing – they do however dance in step with all that is around them whether they can see it with their physical eyes or not. This is what you are learning.

Those who tell you they control things are what the alchemists call "puffers. They are puffed up with their own self-conceit and also afraid if they feel they are not in control. You cannot make the world a "safe, homogenised" place, none of us can. We can learn to live with it and this is a mind-expanding, life-enhancing, experience which continues all the way up to and beyond our death.

Lowerworld is full of surprises, an "Alice Through the Looking-Glass World - full of things which look like things you already think you know and then you find that they are different. This is where many people find they get what they call "nightmares", because the dream world is shocking, it looks the same at first then acts differently so they don't know where they are. They have entered the dream world with a fixed set of preconceptions. We all have preconceptions, ideas of how things are, the problem comes when we refuse to accept that our preconceptions may not be large enough to encompass the reality we experience. The major precept of magical dreaming is Grow Bigger!

Your Notes

Now you have some more experience of the Lowerworld the following exercise will help you find your way around the Upperworld.

EXERCISE UPPERWORLD FAMILIARISATION

Do your usual preparation and open the Interface.

- Turn on the *techyknowledgy*.

- SAY YOUR PURPOSE OUT LOUD, 3 TIMES; "I am here to learn my way around Upperworld"

- FIND YOURSELF IN YOUR SACRED SPACE. Spend a moment or two reacquainting yourself with it. Be at home with your Familiar. When you're BOTH ready, go out ...

- FIND YOURSELF AT YOUR BEGINNING PLACE. Say that you are on an Upperworld Journey and would like to enter. If you are asked for a gift, find it, bring it and enter ...

- SAY YOUR PURPOSE AGAIN ALOUD 3 TIMES; " I am here to learn my way around Upperworld "

- Follow your Familiar UP to Upperworld, they will lead you. There may be someone waiting for you at the top but more likely not, don't have preconceptions. Follow your Familiar, ask questions. Remember – the only stupid question is the one you DIDN'T ask!

- You may be taken to a particular place and the way there can be quite unclear, rather like "Beam me up, Scotty" in Star Trek. You may seem to dematerialise in one place, then re-materialise again in another with no space/time between. This is an Upperworld feature!

- Explore where you find yourself. Take very careful note of everything which happens to you. Keep talking aloud so you have your voice record on tape.

- Gifts from Otherworld are valuable, accept them.

- Don't forget to say thank you when you leave ... even if there seems to be no-one there.

- At the Call Back signal, or before if you are ready, make your way back to your Beginning Place and thank it for helping you!

- FIND YOURSELF BACK IN YOUR SACRED SPACE. Spend time, with your Familiar, recalling, honouring and assimilating the experience. Spend a couple of minutes lying quietly in the foetal position before returning your consciousness to the room.

When you are back, *draw* your journey. This is your first map of Upperworld as it seems to you. As for Lowerworld, don't worry if it doesn't seem like other people's descriptions, it is your perspective and unique to you.

Don't forget to close the Interface and clear your space.

Your Notes

Thoughts and Ideas on
Upperworld

Upperworld, also called Mag Mell, is in the guardianship of Arianrhod, the Lady of the Moon and Stars. Her spiral, spinning tower, called Caer Sidi (pronounced *care shee*), is here.

Arianrhod is the daughter of Beli and Don, the king and queen who began all things in some of the stories. She appears in the stories called "The Children of Don" in the Mabinogion. The stories suggest she is a perilous guardian and teacher as she is very beautiful and also can seem very inhuman in her ways and attitudes. She is concerned with the running of the world and the universe and so individual suffering is not likely to cut much ice with her. She certainly doesn't suffer fools gladly! She will tell you the truth and this may not be what you wish to hear so it may come over as cruel but she will never lie to you and she will tell you where your strengths are.

Arianrhod's story is very much bound up with that of Blodeuwedd and Llew, Gwydion and Math, Mag Mell is also the realm of the Eagle, again this has a relationship to Arianrhod as her son, Llew Llaw Gyffes who is also a sun god, was transformed into his eagle totem when he was mortally wounded by his wife's lover. His father/uncle, Gwydion, found him with the aid of a magical pig (Ceridwen) in the top of a tree dripping gobbets of dead flesh which were being devoured by the pig. Gwydion was able to restore him to human form and life. Llew, Lug, Lugh, are all forms of a word meaning Light.

It is the eagle who offers help from the mountain top so you can reach Upperworld, Mag Mell, the sphere of the Shapers. There is another story of how the Wren came to be the highest flying bird by riding on the back of the eagle and, when the eagle could go no higher, flying up from the eagle's back to go that last bit further.

Upperworld contains the four major archetypes which seem to run through all human traditions in one form or another – Father, Mother,, Daughter, Son. These four form two polarities which enables the current of life to flow.

In many stories the Father depends on the Daughter, the Mother on the Son. Father/daughter stories are those like Yspaddaden and Olwen, and Blodeuwedd. Mother/Son stories are those like Arianrhod and Llew, Ceridwen and Taliesin, and the archetypal Modron (which means mother) and Mabon.

In these stories the child must "win" something from the parent in each case in order to grow into potency. In the case of the daughters it is often to get themselves a husband in spite of the father's objections – so that they can be impregnated on every level and so gain their power and sovereignty. When they do this the father dies.

In the case of the sons they must often "trick" power, name, arms, life itself from the mother and have to undergo severe tests and/or imprisonment in order to become themselves. In these cases the mother does not die but is satisfied in some way by the son's achievement – even if it appears grudgingly.

Mag Mell is the dwelling place of the totems. Celtic tradition has far less information readily available about this realm than the other two and it seems a bright and shadowy place even after many visits. There is always something more, new, different to discover – which usually requires a change of viewpoint from you too.

Mag Mell, Upperworld, is often said to lie "over the sea". I always think of the I Ching saying of "crossing the great water" here as well. This crossing of the sea, the water, is about going out of one's normal element and somewhere else, hence the feeling many people have of being "beamed up". On ordinary sea journeys in the everyday world time can seem to stand still, the effect is similar here. Upperworld is also said to lie "through the circle" "at the world's end and some old ideas about the world were that it was surrounded by an endless sea which washed around and around it forever and was very difficult to cross. Or that it fell in a never ending waterfall over the edge of the world and that if you got too close you would be swept down and lost forever – this also makes me think of "black holes in physics.

As you are going to Upperworld with your Familiar, having asked permission and with some experience of dream travel, you should not get lost or swept away. However, you must always take care – none of these places are "safe" in a way that twenty-first century people seem to like believe things should be!

It is the source of patterns and potential – the patterns which shape the universe and the lives of all that lives within it. Another aspect of the goddess-guardian of this realm is the Spinner, sometimes called Fedelm, the seer who is able to catch the vision of past and future and weave it on the web of space-time. Fedelm is often shown holding a golden spindle and Arianrhod's Spinning Tower is like this too. They weave destiny, consequently they are very good teachers. The guardian does not always appear in just these two forms so expect to meet many different shapes and styles. The Fedelm aspect of the guardian is especially powerful as a dream guide and empowerer.

Upperworld is the place where you find your primary Teacher, learn about your place in the larger scheme of things and how to work with the Guardians. This is very empowering and brings a whole new outlook on life – making it a lot more fun! Upperworld is full of ideas and plans and dreams waiting to become real in the everyday world, not all of them will but the potential is there. As you travel around this realm you will find your own mind expands from contact with things you hadn't yet dreamed of yourself. It really is a place of dreams.

Your Notes

EXERCISE: MIDDLEWORLD FAMILIARISATION

Do your usual preparation and open the Interface.

- Turn on the *techyknowledgy*.

- FIND YOURSELF IN YOUR SACRED SPACE. Spend a moment or two reacquainting yourself with it. Be at home with your Familiar. When you're BOTH ready, go out …

- FIND YOURSELF AT YOUR BEGINNING PLACE. Say that you are on a Middleworld. Journey and would like to enter.

- SAY YOUR PURPOSE AGAIN ALOUD 3 TIMES. " *I am here to learn my way around Middleworld* ".

- Follow your Familiar OUT into the Middleworld. You may find yourself in a place you know well in everyday life. Even if it all looks very like the everyday world you know don't have preconceptions. Keep following your Familiar talk to them, ask questions.

- Explore where you find yourself. Take very careful note of everything which happens to you. Keep talking aloud so you have your voice record on tape.

- Accept gifts, always say thank you when you leave.

- At the Call Back signal, or before if you are ready, make your way back to your Beginning Place … thank it for helping you!

- FIND YOURSELF BACK IN YOUR SACRED SPACE. Spend some time honouring and assimilating the experience. Then return your consciousness to the room and lie on your side quietly in the foetal position for a short while

When you are back, *draw* your journey. This is your first map of the Middleworld as it seems to you. As for the other two worlds, don't worry if it doesn't seem like other people's descriptions, it is your perspective, unique to you. Don't forget to close the directions and clear your space.

Your Notes

Thoughts and Ideas on Middleworld

Middleworld has many guardians – including you! The shapers and empowerers come here too. Some who seem to have a special interest in it from the Celtic lore are Manawyddan who is often known as the Lord of the Sea; Elen of the Ways; Ogma who gives us letters and learning, holds and transmits the lore for us; Barinthos the Ferryman who is like another aspect of Manawyddan and is a psychopomp or guide between the worlds; Gwydion the magician; Sabrina, goddess of the river Severn, also known as Boand in Ireland, and her consort Nechtan, and Math himself.

Middleworld is the place of experience and also the place where we can manifest the ideas and learning we have got from the other two worlds. Through us, it feeds the Upper and Lower worlds as well as being nourished by them. The gods cannot work here on their own they need us as mediums and mediators who can make things real here.

This world, Middleworld, is perhaps the most important place for magical dreamers. It is the place into which you decided to incarnate this time. Yes, *you* decided. Nobody "dumped" on you, you are not a victim of the Powers or their slave. In between lifetimes you did a lot of sorting and thinking and talking with your friends and out of this, between you all, you designed the lifetime that you are now living. For most of us, up to a certain stage of our soul's life – say to the equivalent of early adult-hood – we get a bad dose of amnesia as we are born and do not remember what happened before. Sometimes flashes of memory come past and we are not sure if what we thought was correct. Sometimes the flashes are distorted by our circumstances in this life, our needs and wants, our problems and our joys – yes the good bits can be just as misleading as the bad bits! Magical dreaming can help you overcome the amnesia and be conscious of what you designed your life to be. When you have more of a handle on this you can live it a lot more successfully!

Shamans se journeying to do some of this work, but they more likely journey for specific purposes and for others rather than themselves. Magical dreaming is how you can learn more about yourself, the lifetime you designed for yourself this time and re-finding your friends and guardians across the worlds who can help you fulfil your life's purpose. All this also makes living the actual life a lot more interesting, fun and satisfying than if you are messing about in the dark, so to speak. It helps you have successful relationships with people, animals, plants, your home, your job, your garden, even your politics. All of these things are "sacred", they have their purpose beyond the often narrow view of humans who are not yet ready to dream creatively.

It is this sacred aspect of the world that you will find and work with in Middleworld. It will change your life and your perspective on everything. Even wars, famines and "disasters" will make more sense to you when you know your way around in Middleworld. This can also be very frustrating! You still have to watch non-dreaming politicians making a total cock up of what would otherwise be a perfectly simple situation – and you *have* to stand by silent and not interfere! That is perhaps the hardest part. You *will* find ways in which you can help but they may well be very subtle and not the "white knight on the galloping charger" coming magnificently to the rescue, nor "lady bountiful who knows best" either! You will also learn that your best ways of working magically are actually within the law and system in which you are living, not against it. If you feel you are still at the rebellious stage, wanting to upturn every apple cart in sight and set everyone straight, then ask your Familiar to look after you through this phase and make sure you don't cause too many cock ups with your enthusiasm!

Fluffy bunnies and galloping red setter puppies are gorgeous, beautiful and divine – and bloody useless to the overall Plan!

As you travel more and work in Middleworld you will find yourself able to see, sense and/or feel the strands of the Web. Many people seem to find they have an actual "feel" of the threads in their fingers, like on a spinning wheel or weaving loom, both of which are Celtic symbols as well as used by other traditions.

Sensing these threads you will feel where one is "snagged" or where it needs reconnecting or where there is a tangle. Before you rush in and try to undo the Gordion knot ask your Familiar if this is what you should be doing – sometimes knots are there for a good reason which you may not be able to see straight away. Not everything which at first sight appears wrong is so. Remember how tricky things can seem when you have travelled in Otherworld, how there is no "black and white", no easy way of defining things. You are part of a team now, with your Familiar, your Teacher and all the other Beings you are getting to know in Otherworld. You don't have to do it all by yourself any more, in fact you should not try to do so but always ask the others for their opinion and discuss what you are going to do.

You can take any question which concerns you about anything to do with the everyday world into Middleworld. You will find new and wider perspectives shown to you, sometimes these are not too comfortable as they require you to change your attitudes and prejudices. You may also find that sometimes common current socially acceptable attitudes do not hold up under Otherworld scrutiny and this can be difficult. You still have to live in the everyday world, with its currently acceptable prejudices, which are different from those of twenty years ago and will be different from those held twenty years hence. Somehow you will have to find a way of living with your inner knowledge and still conforming to some extent to public opinion. This is called "keeping your head down"! It does help if you have one or two friends who are also magical dreamers so you can go off down the pub and have a creative whinge together. There is an old psychology adage (probably apocryphal!) which goes "A whinge a day keeps the therapist at bay!".

Perhaps one of the foremost lessons of Middleworld is that you cannot change anything except yourself but in changing yourself you will find the world changes around you.

Your Notes

Some Archetypal Celtic Images

Here are some of the archetypal images in Celtic mythology. You may find yourself in any of these places and sometimes travelling from one to another. Very likely you already know some of them from your dreams.

Well of Segais	Mound	Circle
Crystal Caves	Hollow Hills	Crossroads
Spinning Tower	Arawn's Castle	Enchanted Forest
River Crossing	Abyss	Camelot
Isle of Glas	Endless Planes	Stone Circle

These are some of the major archetypal figures in Celtic mythology which you may already have met and will very likely meet in your dreams.

Ceridwen	Arianrhod	Arawn
Green Man	Lord of the Beasts	Taliesin
Elen of the Ways	Blodeuwedd	Brighid
Llew	Gwydion	Math
Rhiannon	Manawyddan	Merlin

There are many others but this will get you started. It is well worth reading the Mabinogion and Irish Tuatha de Danaan and other stories. There are children's versions, such as Alexander Lloyd's set, which make the stories easier to read than the old versions.

The Many Coloured Land may be full of Beings or completely empty! They come in all shapes and sizes, sometimes indescribable. They may be friends, playmates, tricksters, teachers, healers, Beings who need our help, or with whom we have to fight. All sorts of "things" happen to us in dreams.

Your Notes

132

Brief list of common places

Here are some places where people seem to go regularly in dreams and some thoughts about how you can learn more from and about them. It is not exclusive or complete but just a guide drawn out of my own and my clients' experiences, something for you to begin with. As your dream journal grows so will your personal lexicon of images and their interpretations which may not always coincide with the ones here. That's OK. None of us has the definitive answer – or the world would have ceased evolving long ago and blown itself into a black hole!

CAVES

Caves, holes, tunnels, ways to go inside Mother, Earth. They have lots of bodily significance for most of us relating to ears, noses, mouths, sexual and excretory organs.

Caves are often made by natural processes within the Earth, although some are man-made. Volcanic gasses and the fiery lava of eruptions can create them, or the wearing away by water, or the earth moves and shifts like a sleeper in a dream. Again, you can see the action of the four elements here – gas/air, fire, water, earth – the bodily processes of the Earth. When a volcano erupts it spews up molten rock, ash, gas and steam which then becomes the most fertile place for new life to grow, so it is like a birthing process. When we go down into these caves and tunnels it can be like re-entering a womb and the return journey out of the caves like a rebirth.. Or it may be that the matter we excrete from the cave is stuff that is no longer useful to us – but it will be useful to others in the same way that compost and volcanic ash become fertile soil which nourishes growth.

Caves are often entrances to the Lowerworld, the ancestral realms, the place of the Guardians of power. Strange, shapeshifting. Beings live here. In stories Dragons regularly live in caves lying guard upon their great treasure stores. Jung the psychologist, said of the Lowerworld (he called it the unconscious) *"Here are your dragons, guarding your treasure"*. Just so, we can feel about the caves in the Many Coloured Land.

FORESTS

Forests are often considered primeval places. We talk about the "Wild Wood and the ancient forest. We worry about the preservation and conservation of these ancient places where the original things grew up. They are our heritage. So they are in dreams too.

In the Arthurian myths each of the twelve knights entered the Enchanted Forest at his own place, where no-one had gone before, and carved out his own path through the woods. This is what you have to do in your dreams as you make your way through the Many Coloured Land. In the Arthurian stories the knight always went astray if he followed the path made by another knight and the same goes for you.

Woods and forests are made of three layers, the high top canopy of the oldest and tallest trees, the middle layer of smaller and often shorter-lived trees and the bottom layer of shrubs and bushes. Does this remind you of the three-world make up of Otherworld which is mirrored in the shape of the forest?

The forest doesn't work as a habitat unless it has healthy growth in all three layers and the Many Coloured Land is the same. Your interaction with it helps to keep the forest growing and healthy. When you find yourself within the forest in your dreams remember to ask the forest how it is, if there is anything *it needs of you*, and make sure you act on this when you return to the everyday world.

When you go through the forest see how the paths are – narrow and overgrown, wide and sunlit, winding and full of flowers, dark and full of shadows. How do you feel in there? Do the paths lead you to somewhere or do you get lost? Do you have company, birds, little animals, or are you alone? Talk to your Familiar about these things as you go.

And you can relate the state of the paths (and everything else you meet) to what is happening in your everyday life too. Are you lost there? Is it full of flowers or shadows? Your dreams speak to you about your everyday life *as well as* teaching you about Otherworld. Magical dreaming is about integrating these worlds, seeing the correspondences and how one is reflected in the other.

WATER

Without water we cannot live. This is worth remembering in our dream symbolism. Water carries the life-flow, it is like the blood of the Earth. It is also associated with the feelings and the emotions by many people and this can be appropriate some times but not always so don't get fixed ideas.

What is water? These sort of questions are always so useful to ask, real basic stuff not someone's idea or interpretation. Water is a mixture of two "chemical elements", hydrogen and oxygen. They are very basic, primeval elements, they come early in the Periodic Table, in fact hydrogen is the very first on the list. It's not an equal mix. There are two parts of hydrogen to each one part of oxygen – it's a "triplicity" and Celtic tradition uses this a lot.

Water is "strange" stuff, it has memory, water particles can hold memory of how they have been and where. It has many forms. It can take any shape, flow round any surface, fill up any container. It will hold you up, support you, you can float on it. It will also kill you if you try to breath it – but not always! When you were a baby your lungs were filled with fluid, largely water, and there are scientific means of enabling you to breath while your lungs are filled with water which are used sometimes by divers. Don't try this at home though, the mixtures are very special! So water is a very special liquid.

Water carries nourishment all around the planet. It enables food plants to grow. It carries away and dilutes waste products so that they may become both harmless and useful again. Our own bodies are made up of ninety per cent water.

Water is also beautiful. Imagine rain drops, clouds, waterfalls, lakes, dew on a spider's web, a bowl of water, the light and shade in a puddle, the sound of a river or a stream, waves in the sea, a still calm sea lit by moonlight. The list goes on and on.

And water is fierce, frightening. Imagine waves crashing against rocks, turbulent currents, hail storms, snow drifts, avalanches. Again the list goes on. And in many of these cases water is both beautiful and terrible. It is made up of two different emotions and not always equally – as in its chemical make-up.

If water comes in a dream look at it, observe. What is it doing? How do you feel? Where is it? Is it contained like a bowl or lake or open like the ocean or a massive waterfall? Is it in the bath, toilet, sink, washing up? What are you doing with it? These sort of questions will help you find out what the water is there for, for you, rather than reading a set of re-hashed symbolical meanings from someone else who hasn't had your experiences.

MOUNTAINS

You are probably getting the hang of this by now, that you learn about the "real thing" and then apply that learning to your own dreams. Mountains are the same. Learn about mountains in this world, the naturalist view, and then apply that in symbols to your experiences in the dream worlds.

Mountains are great heaved up masses of the Earth's crust pushed up by two or more continental plates crashing together. Despite our emotional response, the very highest mountains are also the youngest – the old ones have been weathered down to plains. This is very much worth considering when mountains come up in dreams. Is the message about new, young ground which is just being created, for new life, new experience? It may be. Or it may not. There is also a vibrancy about very tall mountains, a feeling which seems to come out of the very earth itself. They are very beautiful. They often make us think of clear, clean air, fantastic views, being above it all and able to see much more of the world than we usually can.

Mountains are the result of strain, two forces opposing each other, pushing in opposite directions. It is because of this pushing that they reach higher and higher into the sky. What does this say to you? Is stress and opposition and pushing valuable sometimes? Is it the catalyst needed to get you to reach out beyond yourself?

Plains and Deserts

We just said that plains are old mountains that have been weathered down. It might make you think of old places that have lost most of their obvious features, hard to distinguish one part from another perhaps. They are old, stable, their features have to be searched for, one has to take time and have patience to find the beauty in them. Those who are young and impatient may be tempted to rush past thinking there's nothing worth bothering with here.

Sometimes you might find yourself crossing what seems like an endless plain. It could be very depressing or it might actually feel very safe as you can see anything coming for miles and you don't have to do anything but keep on walking. When you return from the dream think about your everyday life, does any version of these apply there?

The yellow, Citrinato, phase in alchemy is often spoken of as crossing an endless plain. A time when we seem to have achieved quite a lot but still not really got anywhere. Like in the story at the beginning where the Seeker cannot bring the Faerie gold back across the border without it turning into rocks. In alchemy this is a time of "gestation" which one has to go through. Things are going on inside which you may not realise and your personal self is not able to understand as yet. It's a time for "hanging in there"

Deserts, sand of whatever sort, are harsh for human beings but not for all forms of life. Many have adapted to live within them and would find it very difficult to live anywhere else. If you find yourself in a desert stop still, look about you, wait for one of its inhabitants to turn up and then ask them what they have to tell you or give you. You may well have gone there in order to learn something which you can use in everyday life – symbolically or physically.

Glass is made from super-heated sand. Think about glass. What do you use it for? It's beautiful, useful, dangerous if broken. Think of the transformation it undergoes through fire, from crystalline opaque grains into a clear, misty, coloured, translucent, solid thing. It really is magic.

Flying

Probably everyone has had flying dreams. And also landing-with-a-thud dreams which are very often a sign that you have been travelling out of body and have come back into your body in a clumsy sort of way – like getting both legs down the same trouser leg when getting dressed while half asleep in the morning!

Flying is about being in the air, not touching the ground but flying above it. It is often about being high up though not always. When you find yourself flying in a dream how did this feel at the time? Were you flying under your own power somehow, wings, perhaps? Or were you in an aeroplane, balloon, space ship, kite, rocket? Were you driving or were you being driven? Were you alone? It might also have to do with "transporter" ideas, like in Star Trek.

Had you shapeshifted? Were you a bird or bat or dragon or some other flying creature, no longer in your human form? Were you being carried by one of these creatures? How did you feel about this in the dream? How do you feel about it now? Are these two feelings the same or different? Was the creature one you would expect to fly? Or was it a flying tiger, wolf or cat?

As with all the other examples, does your dream remind you of any stories you've read? Otherworld often use these, especially Faerie stories, myths and legends, to help make themselves understood by us, we find ourselves acting a part in the story in order to understand something in our lives.

How does flying work in the everyday? Why can many birds and insects fly but not people, cats, dolphins? Are the differences here somehow a part of the message we have gone to hear? What are the various types of wing made of in the natural world? Wings are often very beautiful and seem very delicate, sometimes unequal to their apparent task – think of the bumble bee. How much effort is needed by birds or insects in order to fly, how much food, of what quality? What are a bird's bones like and how does this help them to fly? Do insects have bones? What does this say to you of your own everyday life?

Learn about flying in this world, the naturalist view, and then apply that in symbols to your experiences in the dream worlds.

Eyes

Lots of people find themselves, often quite suddenly, in a place that is full of eyes. Usually just eyes, no heads, no bodies, and they are all looking at you. There are lots of possibilities here, the eyes as the window to the soul is one. What can you not see? How are you seeing things? The eyes are looking at you.

One thing I've found helpful is to ask the eyes if I may see through them, see what they are seeing, view myself their way. This involves you in a bit of shapeshifting as you have to move a part of your consciousness out of yourself and into the eyes.

Do not do this until you have done and feel confident with the exercises on shapeshifting. If you find yourself here before you have had a chance to practice tell the eyes you will be back and ask your Familiar to help you return out of the dream and to your Sacred Space again. Don't try and "tough it out", it really isn't worth it and you won't get any credit – except for being an idiot. Discretion is *always* the better part of gung ho.

HEADS AND FACES

Heads and faces are very similar to eyes but have the advantage that, usually, they can speak so you don't have to do shapeshifting in order to learn. There are many Celtic stories of "heads", Bran is one of the best known, who advised, gave out the lore, wisdom and so was often consulted.

The heads of enemies and of previous rulers or wise men would be cut off and kept in some way. They were also used as guardians, stuck on poles around the edge of the stockade perhaps, where their staring visages would defy other enemies and cry out if it saw one coming. You may find these story-images appropriate if you find yourself in the place of heads.

BUTCHER'S SHOP

This is a strange one and you may find it scary. It deals with the symbols of eating and being eaten which come in dreams and Otherworld work. About losing, giving up part of ourselves which has been very useful in the past but is no longer any good to us now. Many people are loath to give their old habits up so some friendly monster, Familiar, or other Being comes along and chops it off!

You might go into the butchers shop and find parts of yourself hanging up there, maybe appearing older or younger, or you-at-work, or you-the-seductress. These can be parts you need to *feed on* at the moment – maybe you need to be a seductress just now but had been feeling guilty or afraid of it. So your Familiar and/or Teacher decides to do a bit of "shock tactics" to get you to move out a rut. At other times they are things you have been hanging on to for too long and the only way to rid you of them is to show you the butchers shop.

If you don't understand what the message then ask. Ask your Familiar – that is at least partly why you have asked them to come with you after all, and they do know. Much better than I do in this book. What I am giving you here is the result of experience, my own and those of others who are willing to share their dreams through this book. But your first port of call is always your Familiar and then your Teacher. Before me. Before this book.

Hospital Waiting Room or Foyer

This scenario often occurs when you are working with people who are dying or, occasionally, when you go to meet someone who is not incarnate, It is as though you cannot go too far in that particular direction and a place is provided for you to meet where the energies are suitable for both of you. Sometime this happens when you go to meet your Teacher. It almost seems as if they have been busy somewhere else, where you cannot go, and they "pop out" of the lab or board meeting or wherever for a minute to meet with you. I've even had a "tea break" with mine!

The meaning behind "not able to go further" is to protect you.. Until you have "strengthened your fibres as Castaneda used to say, you can only cope with energy up to a certain level before you get "fried". Otherworld does not want to fry you, so they give you a safe place. The work you are doing here will help to "strengthen" you but all of us have our limits as long as we are in human form and even after that. It all depends on how much you've grown. There's no disgrace in not knowing everything – very few Beings do!

Your Notes

Glossary

ACTIVE DAY-DREAMING – Doing , being creative, taking part, making choices within a dream-like situation while one is "awake". One is conscious of the room or place one is in and, at the same time, conscious of the dream-world. In two places at once.

AIR – One of the four elements, corresponds to the *thinking* mental part of ourselves.

AKASHA – The place of records. We can relate it to Jung's 'unconscious' and quantum's 'state of potential'.

ALCHEMY – Ancient, secret, practice and lore. Alchemy is about how the world is made. See bibliography.

ALDER – One of the sacred trees, associated with Bran.

ANCESTORS – Not necessarily your physical genetic forebears. Ancestry comes through the soul and your soul family are far more likely to make contact through dreams than your physical ancestors, although they may. You usually find that the physical ancestor who contacts you is also a member of your soul family.

ANCHOR – Some thing or idea which grounds you, connects you to the Earth. Very important, without this you won't function effectively in your everyday life, job, relationships.

ANIMAL – A being with whom you share this planet. Animals are different from humans but not lesser. They help us learn equality. When we treat animals with as much respect as we do our loved ones then we begin to have a good relationship with the world.

ANNWN – The kingdom of Arawn, King of the Underworld. This is a place of potential, rather like the Akasha. It holds the cornucopia, the horn of plenty, from which you can draw. It is a place of beauty, colour, light and shadow. The essence, spirit, of everything on the Earth lives there.

ARCHETYPE– An 'original concept', idea behind something, pattern.

ARIANRHOD'S SPINNING TOWER– Arianrhod's tower is like a spinning vortex, it spins so fast it appears to be still. It is like T.S. Eliot's line *"at the still point of the turning world.* It has some correlations to the Tower in the tarot, but don't get limited by what you know of this, Arianrhod's Tower is a very large concept.

ARAWN – The King of the Underworld in Celtic lore. A powerful figure, often crowned with horns, he rides a white horse and has a pack of white hounds with red ears and eyes who are also called the Yell Hounds,, or

Gabriel Hounds. He is also the 'righter of wrongs', guardian of the beasts and keeper of the cauldron of plenty.

ARAWN'S CASTLE – A bright, dark shadowy place, full of the unexpected. It is not evil but it isn't one which is designed to be 'human friendly'! It is geared to provide experience and adventure and, of course, it was built to house its owner – who is not human!

ASK – The age old and ageless first principle of magic. You ask, you do not command. It's part of learning equality!

ASLEEP – This can mean physical sleep, resting the body and allowing the unconscious mind to work freely. It can also mean being *asleep to the wider reality*, to the world of magic. Everyone wakes to this in their own good time. There is an old adage *"never wake the sleeper"* meaning never try to give someone knowledge they haven't asked you for. Never know best, never know first!

ASTRAL – The realm of the *feelings*, emotions, one of the subtle bodies which makes up our personality. It is a part of this world, the Earth. Astral travel, much vaunted, is not travel to the realms of spirit but the same thing one does when taking LSD or other hallucinatory drugs.. You travel indeed, but only within the 'shadowlands' of the real places. Spirit travel and journeying are something very different. The astral is like a training pool, where you can learn to swim, not too deep and with lots of steps and hand holds. Spirit travel on the other hand is rather like going into space, if your space suit breaks, that's it!

AUTOMATON – Something which looks and functions like a human being but isn't properly human. The physical body is an automaton which is brought to life by the soul. Automatons should be respected, without our bodies our souls would have no means of working here on Earth.

AWAKE – Being physically awake as opposed to asleep. Also being spiritually aware, at least partially. Awake to new things which may not seem logical or reasonable at first. If you are not awake in this sense it is impossible for you to learn anything.

AXIS – Either vertical or horizontal. Something which help us define the world and ourselves by giving us up/down, east/west/north/south.

BEFRIENDING – Becoming friends with someone or something. It can only be done when you are able to see yourself as equal-but-different from the other. While you see yourself as either superior or inferior you can never befriend.

BEGINNING PLACE – A known point on you inner map which then enables you to go on and find other places.

BEHAVE APPROPRIATELY – Behaving in the right way for the time, place and situation you find yourself in. Not working from a set of rigid rules but being awake and aware to each individual situation and working with that.

BEINGS – A wide term which encompasses just about anything. Never close your mind to what a 'being' can look like, say or do.

BETWEEN LIGHTS, BETWEEN THE TWO LIGHTS – The 'two lights' are the Sun and Moon. Between them is the 'twilight' which is like the interface, where neither sun nor moon holds sway. It is a magical time and place which is held and created for us by the two major influences in our sky. The word 'twilight' is a contraction of 'between the two lights'.

BIG PICTURE – Our view of the world is only ever as large as we are comfortable with at that time. If we are evolving then our picture grows too. Our soul has a much bigger picture of life, the universe and everything than our personal self. The personal picture grows with experience, both everyday and magical, so it gets a bit closer to the Big Picture.

BODY – The physical body. It can also mean the whole of the personal self, the physical, emotional and thinking parts.

BRAIN – The physical lump of grey matter, the "little grey cells" of Poirot! It looks a bit like a gone off cauliflower but is the most intricate labyrinth we know. The brain does the physical stuff, fires synapses and such like. The mind is another place.

BRIDGE – Something which helps us cross from one place to another, often over some 'dangerous chasm', which might be a difficult idea, new concept or physical place. We can build our own as well as use those built by others who have gone before.

BRIGANTIA – The 'goddess of the land' of Britain, from whose name the word comes. She is associated with the Irish Brighid and has the same attributes.

BRIGHID – Keeper of the sacred fire, patron of Smiths (makers), Poets and Healers. Goddess of inspiration. Her sacred time is Imbolc, 31st January.

BRITAIN – Ancient island, known to the Greeks and well before that. In old stories it's called the 'Island of the Mighty' which doesn't really refer to physical prowess but the wise ones and the lore which was kept here. Orpheus came to Britain to learn and also to help build Stonehenge, so the old stories say. It is also known as Merlin's Precinct or land.

BUILDING – To make something real from a pattern or idea. Manifest, hard-copy, in the flesh.

BURNT NORTON – A very deep, spiritual poem by T.S. Eliot.

CAUSAL – Reason behind something, cause, power which makes it happen.

CENTRE – The point within one's self where you are you. This goes for any being or planet or virus or particle. The place from which things flow outwards into the world.

CHANGE – Usually a difficult process! Once a change has occurred you can never return to the former state.

CHANT – A form of ritual singing. Can be wordless but will have a rhythm and form. It is often repetitive and can induce a trance-like state in the singer and the listeners.

CHOICE – The ability to differentiate and to decide between one thing and another. A sign of being 'grown up'! Taking responsibility and not apportioning blame.

CIRCLE – Magical form, without beginning or end. Signifies spirit.

CITIFIED – Conforming to the cultural mores of city-life. This can mean cut off from the natural world. Many city dwellers have only a restricted contact with the other creatures with whom we share this planet and come to believe that their own mores (ideas) are the only 'correct' ones. A difficult place!

CLAN – In magical work a 'clan' is a grouping of like souls as well as those of one blood. It can also have more restrictive meanings which exclude others – this is not so good.

CLEARING – Clearing yourself of where you have been. Like after watching a film and the lights go up. If you were really into the film you have to take a minute or two to get back into the 'real world'.

COLLECTIVE, COLLECTIVE UNCONSCIOUS – This word is often used along with the Unconscious and associated with Jung. In those terms it is about the whole mass of human consciousness and the potential of all humanity. In this book we take that further and include all Life, not just humans, in this idea.

COMMITMENT – Putting your heart and soul into something, often entails taking risks because you don't know the outcome, If you don't have the ability to do this then life gets very stale!

CONFUSED – A normal state for most of us! Try to get over any ideas you may have that it's 'wrong' to be confused. It just means you don't know. If you expect to know everything, always, all the time you will have a very unhappy life.

CONSCIOUSNESS – A sense of *knowing*, not dependant on knowledge and often coming quite apart from that, without reason. A very profitable state to be in. It can also be uncomfortable until you get accustomed. You hear, see, feel far more than when you are unconscious and this can be painful and confusing. To be conscious successfully you have to learn the boundaries between self and not-self, what is 'me' and what is 'not me'.

CONTACT – To become aware of something beyond your own current idea of it. To expand your idea of something.

CONTAINER – The body is a container for the soul. The Earth is a container for the Life that lives here. The Solar System is a container for this star and its set of planets. The Milky Way is the container for the Solar System – etc.

CONTEMPLATE – different from thinking. Instead of 'trying to make sense' you just allow the experience to flow through you, watching, noting the new shapes, ideas, colours, forms that you see as it does so. Knowing and sense come of themselves without you having to force anything. It's a very important part of magical working. But you have to stay focused and not drift off into the astral or you end up with a real mish-mash instead of an answer.

CONTINUITY – Learning to know that all time is 'now', alternate realities is a useful way of getting a handle on this difficult concept. Death becomes a process, a mode of change, rather than an ending. A change of cosmic address as Bob Toben puts it!

CONTROL – Usually we all like to be in control and are afraid if we feel we lose it. In magical work we learn to give up this small and personal idea of control so that it can grow and we can make contact with other beings.

CREATE – A truly magical process, full of risk and responsibility and the chance for us to get it all wrong! When we create something it springs out of our minds and into reality. We never are able to know all the potential, things have a life of their own, but we do it anyway. Learning consciousness helps to lessen the risks of harm to our fellow beings!

DAY-DREAMING – Many of us will recall being told off for this! It's a very practical and creative thing to do. Many scientific discoveries have been made when the scientist was 'day-dreaming'. Ursula K Le Guin, in some of her novels, uses the term 'far-fetching' – this gives another slant on it. When we day-dream we are fetching 'knowing' from afar, maybe out beyond consciousness.

DEDICATING – Offering and committing to something.

DIALOGUE – Talking 'with', as opposed to talking 'to'!

DIRECTIONS – In this book we talk of North, East, South, West, Above, Below, Within.

DOOR – A 'device' which defines a place, a boundary.

DREAM JOURNAL – Like a diary. Journal means 'day book'. With a dream journal you don't have to have every single day in it – although it's good to be regular. Entries will vary in length, may include drawings.

DREAM MAKER – Your teacher in the dream world.

DREAM TIME –Australian native peoples way of speaking of the worlds.

EARTH – This planet. One of the four elements which go to make up all life.

EAST – One of the four directions, associated with Air, morning, sun-rise, new-ness, the *thinking* process, mental body and the mind.

ELEMENTS – The four elements, Earth, Air, Fire, and Water, which correspond to the parts of ourselves, Earth-physical, Air-thinking, Fire-soul and spirit, Water-feelings and emotions.

EMOTIONS – The part of ourselves which feels. E-motion is about that which enables movement. Our feelings help us to move and change and grow, they are the motive and motor power.

ENABLING – Making possible. The opposite of stopping something.

ENCHANT – To sing into life, en-chant. The magic in things.

ETHERIC – Blueprint of the physical world and your physical body.

EVERYDAY WORLD – What most people consider 'reality', part of but not the whole, which extends beyond the common five senses. Even scientifically this is true, consider the concepts of quantum mechanics and mathematics.

FAERIE – A name for a part of Otherworld, not by any means the whole of Otherworld. The place of the elementals and devas who take care of the plants, animals and minerals of the world. These beings have been called 'fairies'.

FAERIE GOLD – Riches which become insubstantial when we try to bring them back into the everyday world from faerie. Eventually we learn how to transport them across the boundary successfully, without them losing their substance.

FAERIE QUEEN – The sovereign lady of Faerie.

FAMILIAR – Your "familiar spirit". It's an old British term for what is often called a "power animal". The familiar can have a physical presence in the everyday world where power animals are wholly of Otherworld. You have heard of the witch and her black cat or toad or other creature but they are not "evil", they are our friends.

FEED – To nourish. In magic feeding is far more than just eating three square meals a day. It's an "exchange". Both Upper and Lower worlds need stuff from Middle world in order to grow and human beings are the means by which they can get this. In return Upper and Lower Worlds give to Middle. We too can feed on the magic.

FEELINGS – One of Jung 's four functions. As well as the everyday usage *feelings* has a specific meaning here as well. It refers to the astral/ emotional part of ourselves and is the part which is best able to access the astral plane which relates to the element water.

FINDING – Uncovering something which has been hidden, something which was always there but you didn't know until now. Finding is something we hope to do every day of our lives!

FIRE – One of the four elements. It relates to the Intuition and the Soul, that part of ourselves which reaches across the worlds and continues beyond the physical death of our bodies. The other elements, earth, air and water, relate very much to this Earth, fire goes beyond, symbolised by the Sun which is the means by which Life occurs on this planet.

FOCUS – Without focus there is no magic and no magical dreaming. It is one of the first things to learn, to keep on target, not to be distracted whatever the emotional pulls that come from outside. It can make you seem hard and it can make you unpopular as you are not always at your friends' beck and call.

FRAME – Like skeleton, something which holds a thing in shape, enables it to keep its form. Your Dreamweb needs this.

GATEWAY – A crossing-place from the everyday into the dream world, Otherworld, And a return-place at the end of your dream.

GODS & GODDESSES – Beings which are more than ourselves. And less. Gods and goddesses don't live in the everyday world as we do, because they can't. They use us to help them in their work and we ask them to help us in ours. Exchange.

GUARDIAN – are those beings who look after others. For instance, there is the Cat Guardian who looks after all cats, or the Oak Guardian, or the Slug Guardian, or the Amethyst Guardian, or the Motor Vehicle Guardian, or the Rose Guardian. They can also be the guardians of places such as the guardian of Stonehenge, Ayers Rock, Snowdon, Loch Ness. And they can be the guardian of the place where you live. Any place which is a whole, has a boundary, grows a guardian. Try contacting the guardian of your home.

GUIDE – Someone who has gone the way you wish to go and knows the way, will lead you helpfully. Sometimes you too will be a guide.

HEALERS – Those who help others to be what they truly are, regardless of whether this is painful to the healer. They do not necessarily cure illness, they know that illness and death are not necessarily "bad" even if they are frightening.

HEARING – A very important function! And one we are often not very good at! To hear properly is to hear without knowing, making assumptions or rushing in before whoever is speaking has finished. To hear what the person is actually saying and not what you think they are saying or want them to say! How good at hearing are you?

HUMANKIND – The youngest species on Planet Earth. We certainly behave like it! Everything else on the planet has been here a lot longer than us but we are often too arrogant to listen to it. Humans are also the main link between the planet and the Otherworlds, via dreams.

HYPNOGOGIC STATE – The threshold between waking and sleeping.

IMAGE – Usually people think of these as visual, pictures, and so they often are. However, if you have difficulty with pictures it may be your images come to you better through sound or scent or touch or taste. Don't rule out anything.

IMBOLC – The goddess Brighid, Lady of Fire and Inspiration has her Fire Festival of Imbolc on 31st January/1st February, the Willow month.

INCUBATE – The process of holding something within a womb-like structure and bringing it to fruition. Often this is a warm, secret and sacred place.

INITIATES – Those who are able, amongst other things, to dream consciously. They can retain conscious awareness as they pass into and out of sleep.

INSPIRATION – Literally, to breath in, to take in air and so stay alive. To take in *knowing*, ideas, images, from Otherworld via our dreams. This helps us to become alive more fully.

INSTRUMENTS – See also paraphernalia. Your Dreamweb is one of your instruments. As you make it you invest it with your own power.

INTERACT – Working *with* … Not just being an observer but getting involved, taking part, joining, sharing, exchanging.

INTERCONNECTEDNESS – The web of Life, the way no one of us can live without the others – and not just people. People need all the other beings that we share this planet with in order to live.

INTERFACE – The place where worlds meet and overlap so that one is in two places at the same time. If you want to follow this up further in the "everyday" world go an look for books on quantum mechanics – see Further Inspiration "The Dancing Wu Li Masters" and "Einstein for Beginners".

INTUITION – One of Jung's four functions. It relates to the element of fire and to the soul.

INVESTS – Fills, deposits, commits. Offer to the future.

JOURNEY – In this book to "journey" is to travel between and through worlds.

JUMP-GATE – From a sci-fi series, Babylon 5. A means of going instantaneously from one place to another. Dreamweb.

JUNG – One of the leading psychologists of the 20th Century. Read "Jung for Beginners" for more about him. Or his books.

KNOWING – This is quite different from "knowledge"! Try this … if I throw a bucket of water over you then you *know* you are wet, it's not a matter for belief or doubt. This is what knowing is.

LABYRINTHS – A labyrinth, in general, has a way in and a way out. A maze may or may not lead you out again.

LIFE – A force, or energy, which continually changes and grows including more and more within itself as it becomes more knowing.

LIFE'S CONTINUITY – Life doesn't end just because our physical bodies die. By the time you reach the age of twenty-one just about every cell in your body has died and been replaced three times – yet "you" are still there … !

LISTENING – See hearing.

LOGICAL MIND – The part of the mind which thinks in a linear fashion and very useful it is too! Try driving with only your pattern-forming mind and see how long before you have an accident!

LORE – The pattern, web, story of life as it is "known". Often this is handed down through story, song, pictures in each culture. When we look at the stories we often find them remarkably similar. Perhaps the Lore is all one?

LOWERWORLD – The place of the ancestors. Jung might call it the Unconscious. Eastern mystics might call it the Akasha. Explore it for yourself, it's where your friends and family are.

MAGIC – The ability to do things the logical mind says are impossible. Everyday miracles like seeds germinating, the sun rising.

MANIFESTATION – The process of bringing a thought-idea through the realm of dreams so that it comes to life in the everyday world. Also called "making".

MANY COLOURED LAND – The worlds we go to in dreams.

MAP – A diagrammatic means of finding one's way around. The map rarely looks like the actual place but it somehow enables us to think in the abstract and find where we are and how to get where we're going. Old adage – "*the map is not the country*".

MAZE – See labyrinth.

MENTAL (PLANE) – It relates to the element of air, it's about thinking and the intellect. One of Jung's four functions is *thinking*.

MIDDLEWORLD – The spiritual counterpart of our everyday world.

MISTAKES – One of the most effective ways of learning! An old adage says – "*A person who has never made a mistake has never made anything!*".

MOON – The light of the night. The silver lantern. The one who controls the waters and so the feelings, astral plane. One of the "two lights" which enable the twilight, the interface, the place between worlds, to be.

MYTHOLOGY – A tale, or set of tales, which is non-logical and often not-provable in the ordinary sense, yet it holds us in a way which logical things do not. It is a part of the soul and speaks to us through our intuition and our souls.

NAVIGATE – Find your way from one place or world to another and back again.

NEXUS – A point where ways come together or from which they go out.

NORTH – One of the four directions, associated with Earth, night, ancestors, darkness, womb, the physical and etheric body, and physical sensation. [transposes to south for those in the southern hemisphere]

OBSERVER – A name for the soul-part, the one who watches and observes, who inhabits our physical body, works with our feelings and our thinking.

OTHERWORLD – An overview term for all the worlds other than our everyday one.

PARAPHERNALIA – The magicians tools. You probably know of such things as wands, scrying mirrors, crystal balls, broomsticks. These are all "focusing devices" for the magician to enable her/him to work magic. They help but are not essential to the very experienced mage, but for all the rest of us they're invaluable!

PASSENGER – One who is just carried along, doesn't participate, allowing others to do everything for them. Not a magical dreamer!

PATTERN – Patterns, things which come or fit together in some "knowable wholeness". All beings have this pattern-knowing ability in some form, look at the way crystals form. We are pattern formers, pattern holders, pattern recognisers, pattern shapers and so is everything around us. We learn to recognise this.

PERSPECTIVE – Our perspective changes depending on where we are. It is our view of the world from where we stand, physically, mentally and from our soul-growth state. It changes as we grow and move. It is how we see the world, now.

POTENTIAL – The possibility for something. An idea before it becomes an actuality.

POWERS – beings who are our teachers and who bring the world into being through their ideas. Some call them gods.

RELATIONSHIP – Your ability to interact successfully and creatively with other beings – sometimes of your own species but also those who are not human and not incarnate as you are.

RESPECT – An "equal eyes" relationship with everything else. Not considering yourself to be either better or worse than the other you are working with. Not getting into either a "parental" or a "child" role but working adult to adult.

RESPONSIBLE – Being active and taking on your own part in any situation, not being a "victim" or "helpless" and thereby dumping everything onto someone else. It also means taking on board your own power and your ability to be hurt and to give hurt.

RITUAL – A choreographed way of doing something which helps to focus your attention and transport you across the worlds.

SACRED SPACE – Sometimes called the temenos, your own space within Otherworld and the Interface where you can be completely alone and safe. It is very important to have such a place if you want to work magically and it's also very helpful for everyday life too.

SEEKER – An old name for the aspiring apprentice who goes out looking for his or her magical master. Read the old fairy stories and you'll see them everywhere.

SELF – The Self, with a capital "S", was the word Jung and others used for the non-personal part of one's self. It is also called the soul but not too often by psychologists who seem to have great difficulty in believing in souls despite the fact that the word "psyche" in Greek means soul!

SENSORY, SENSATION – One of Jung's four functions, the physical body, sensory self which is able to know sensations, physical touching, wind on the skin, fur, slippery, etc.

SHAMAN – One who knows, who is able to travel consciously across the worlds. A mediator.

SMITHCRAFT – The art of making. In the British tradition the great smith is Weyland. He holds a doorway between the worlds and through the arts of fire gives form to metals, which are what the earth is made of, so he gives form to the Earth. The patroness of smiths is Brighid.

SOUL AXIS – The vertical axis between heaven and Earth.

SOUTH – One of the four directions, associated with Fire, mid-day, the sun's highest point in the sky, culmination, bringing to light, manifestation, the intuition and soul. [transposes to north for those in the southern hemisphere]

STAR-GATE – See jump-gate.

SYMBOL – Another focusing device. Something which signifies something else without necessarily looking like it. Symbols usually reach right into us and touch something, our soul, which another picture might not.

TALISMAN – In some ways this might be like your familiar but it isn't necessarily an animal, it might be a shape, colour, sound, something quite abstract. People wear pentagrams, crosses, stars, circles, all sorts of things which they think of as their "lucky charms". The talisman may be like this but it is also able to speak and advise – if you bother to ask it!

TEACHERS – Beings from Upperworld who take on the task of teaching us through our dreams and in other ways.

THANKING – Rarely remembered but very important part of magical working! Otherworld will consider you childish if, like a child, you rush off with your learning and gifts without bothering to say thank you.

THE TREE – The Tree of Wisdom and Tradition in the British tradition and Yggdrasil from the Norse. It also appears in the eastern mythos. The tree holds up the world and is what all the worlds are built around.

TWO LIGHTS – The sun and the moon, the light of day and the light of night. Twilight is the time between the two lights when neither sun nor moon rules. (See also Between Lights)

THINKING – One of Jung's four functions, related to Air.

THRESHOLD – The place where you cross from one place to another. Often thresholds have guardians who won't let you cross until you are ready, and unlikely to cause harm in the world into which you will step. The guardians have a two-fold job, to protect us from getting hurt and, perhaps even more important, to protect Otherworld from us! Well known guardians are Cerebrus, the three headed dog who guards Hades, dragons, the Sphinx and many others. Read the stories to find them.

TRADITION – A set of lore, tales, beliefs, through which a particular group of people view the world, their perspective. There are many and all are valid.

TRANCE – A state where one can travel between worlds. However there are two sorts of trance, one where you have no control over what is happening and the other where you consciously decide. The latter is much safer!

TRANSPERSONAL – Beyond the personal perspective towards the soul's perspective.

TRANSPORTER ROOM – See jump-gate.

TRICKSTERS – These are teachers. They have our welfare and growth at heart although it often doesn't seem like this at the time. Humans are such awkward beings that they often need to be tricked into doing things as they are far to stubborn to change of their own free will! Some famous "tricksters" are Hermes, Coyote, Fox, Loki. But all the gods have this aspect to them.

TS ELIOT – A British poet of the first half of the 20ᵗʰ century.

UPPERWORLD – The place of ideas and potential. Assagioli might call it the superconscious. Eastern mystics might call it the Void. Explore it for yourself, it's where your teachers are.

WALK BETWEEN THE WORLDS – To consciously move between the everyday world and the land of dreams.

WATCHER – See Observer.

WATER – One of the four elements, corresponds to the *feeling* part of ourselves.

WEST – One of the four directions, associated with Water, evening, sunset, old things, the feeling process, the astral body.

WITHIES – Long straight stems of the willow tree, very bendable.

Further Inspiration

The Mabinogion

Parsifal & the Holy Grail

Anderson Hans Complete Fairy Tales

Bach Richard Jonathan Livingstone Seagull Illusions Bridge Across Forever; One

Baines Chris How to make a Wildlife Garden

Bates Brian The Way of Wyrd

Beningfield Gordon Beningfield's Woods - magical artist's view

Blake William Anything - he was in touch

Briggs Katharine A Dictionary of Fairies.

Campbell Joseph The Hero with a Thousand Faces

Capra Fritjof The Tao of Physics

Carroll Lewis Alice in Wonderland; Through the Looking Glass; Hunting of the Snark

Cooper J C An Illustrated Encyclopaedia of Symbols

Dadd Richard All his fairy paintings - done from life!

Dames Michael The Avebury Cycle; The Silbury Treasure; Mythic Ireland

Dawkins Peter Arcadia

Delaney Frank The Celts

Donne John particularly his love poems

Eliot T S Four Quartets & Collected Poems

Fitzgerald John Anster Faerie pictures

Fortune Dion The Sea Priestess; Moon Magic

Fraser J G The Golden Bough

Gallico Paul Jennie; Snow Goose

Garner Alan any of his stories - all superb, also his poetry

Graeme Kenneth Wind in the Willows

Graves Robert The Greek Myths; The White Goddess

Grimm Brothers Fairy Tales - magical, wonderful

Hamilton Geoff Paradise Gardens

Herbert Frank Dune

Herrigel Eugen Zen and the Art of Archery

Hughes Ted Crow, The Hawk in the Rain

Icon Books Einstein for Beginners; Newton for Beginners; Jung for Beginners; Universe for Beginners

Lang Lloyd & Jennifer Art of the Celts

Lao Tzu Tao Te Ching

le Guin Ursula Left Hand of Darkness; Earthsea Trilogy; The

Dispossessed; City of Illusion

Lewis C S The Narnia Cycle; That Hideous Strength

Matthews Caitlin Singingthe Soul Back Home; In Search of Woman's Passionate Soul; Singing the Soul Back Home; Mabon & the Mysteries of Britain; Arthur & the Sovereignty of Britain

Matthews John Taliesin - Shamanism & the Bardic Mysteries in Britain & Ireland; Robin Hood

Matthews John & Caitlin The Western Way

McBeath Alastair Sky Dragons & Celestial Serpents

Milne A A Winnie the Pooh; The House at Pooh Corner

Rackham Arthur Faerie pictures

Renault Mary The KingMust Die; The Bull from the Sea; The Mask of Apollo; Firefrom Heaven; The Last of the Wine

Reps Paul Zen Flesh, Zen Bones

Rola Stanislas Klossowski de Alchemy- the Secret Art

Roob Alexander Alchemy& Mysticism

Stewart Mary The Crystal Cave; The Hollow Hills; The Last Enchantment

Stewart R J The Merlin Tarot

Tepper Sherri S The Jinian Footseer cycle

Toben Bob Space-time & Beyond - out of print, hunt for it

Tolkein JRR The Hobbit; The Lord of the Rings; Farmer Giles of Ham; Gawain and the Green Knight

Tolstoy Nicholas The Quest for Merlin

Wombwell Felicity The Goddess Changes

Yeats W B all his poems

Zelazny Roger Everything, but particularly – Lord of Light; Creatures of Light and Darkness; A Night in Lonesome October

Zukav Gary The Dancing Wu Li Masters

CPSIA information can be obtained
at www.ICGtesting.com
Printed in the USA
BVHW030256131218
535537BV00001B/126/P